LIVE THE
LET-GO
LIFE

—

STUDY GUIDE

ALSO BY JOSEPH PRINCE

For more information on these books and other inspiring resources,
visit JosephPrince.com.

LIVE THE
LET-GO
LIFE

STUDY GUIDE

Breaking Free from Stress,
Worry, and Anxiety

JOSEPH PRINCE

INTERNATIONAL BESTSELLING AUTHOR

New York • Nashville

FaithWords
Hachette Book Group
1290 Avenue of the Americas
New York, NY 10104
faithwords.com
twitter.com/faithwords

First Edition: October 2017

FaithWords is a division of Hachette Book Group, Inc. The FaithWords name and logo are trademarks of Hachette Book Group, Inc.

The publisher is not responsible for websites (or their content) that are not owned by the publisher.

The Hachette Speakers Bureau provides a wide range of authors for speaking events. To find out more, go to www.hachettespeakersbureau.com or call (866) 376-6591.

Literary development: Lance Wubbels Literary Services, Bloomington, Minnesota.

ISBN: 978-1-4789-7035-4

Printed in the United States of America
10 9 8 7 6 5 4 3 2

CONTENTS

INTRODUCTION

It feels like our world today is spinning faster on its axis than ever before and picking up momentum with each passing day. Many factors add to our frantic pace of life. There are unending daily to-do lists. New demands are arising in a rapidly changing workplace, and almost every industry has been confronted by disruption. Many are struggling with the need to keep up with new knowledge and to be retrained or redeployed in order to stay relevant, while juggling the demands of marriage, parenting, and church. All this is happening amid a backdrop of very real threats of superbugs and terror in our everyday lives. On top of all this, the immediacy of real-time communications through various mediums such as text messages, Snaps, and WhatsApp group chats has also created a new normalcy of demands on us.

It's not hard to see why so many people today are experiencing stress, worry, and anxiety attacks. Unfortunately, these aren't simply innocent states of emotion—they can insidiously develop into chronic depression, psychosomatic illnesses, and lead to self-destructive behaviors. No one should ever underestimate the debilitating power of stress, which has been called a "silent killer," with its long list of serious consequences.

At its very core, stress is about demands—demands that we can neither keep up with nor satisfy. But the Lord's grace is all about supply! I want to teach you how to walk in a greater measure and depth of the Lord's supply, and practical ways to allow His supply in your life to flow unabated. Stress, worry, and anxiety choke God's supply of favor, wisdom, and good success. The more you learn to let go of your anxieties, the more you will see His supply flow. I have no doubt that as you use this study guide, you will be greatly encouraged and strengthened as chapter by chapter, you learn and begin to practice powerful scriptural truths that deal with stress.

Here's the good news: Today, even if worry, anxiety, and stress have become your longtime companions, they no longer have to rule your life. Instead, you can learn how to trust the Lord to handle your every care. You can receive hope and strength to face each new day confident and unafraid in His unfailing and personal love for you. You can break free of the shackles of the past, you can look forward to the future, and you can enjoy the present despite its demands.

Even if you don't feel like you're under much stress, I hope you'll give attention to the questions and truths this study guide will point you to. Don't wait until it's too late, and the stress in your life has reached destructive levels. The time to overcome stress, anxiety, depression, and fear is now. I pray that you'll discover the power of letting go today and begin to walk in the freedom of a life at rest in the Father's love.

My dear reader, you were not designed by God to live under stress; you were called to live the life of rest. The life of rest is a life of victory. Come with me, my friend, and let's start living the *let-go life*—a quality life free from stress, worry, and anxiety!

HOW TO USE
THIS STUDY GUIDE

I'm delighted that you've chosen to use this study guide that was written as a companion to my book *Live the Let-Go Life: Breaking Free from Stress, Worry, and Anxiety*. This study guide will show you how to successfully overcome stress and anxieties that result from the everyday demands and pressures of modern living. Through prayerfully going over the questions here, may you discover how you were not designed by God to live under stress, but called to live the life of rest!

This study guide has been created so that it lends itself to self-study or personal development, as well as small-group study or discussion, say in a care group or book club setting. Whichever the purpose you have in mind, you'll find ample opportunities to personally encounter the Lord as you take time to study and meditate on His Word, and hear His Spirit speak and minister His love, grace, and peace to your heart and mind.

The format of each chapter is simple and user-friendly. To get the most out of each chapter, it would be best to first read the corresponding chapter in *Live the Let-Go Life*. That will give you more background and understanding. If you're not sure how to answer a certain question that is based on a teaching in the parent book, there is a helpful answer guide at the back you can refer to. It covers all the questions except for those that require a personal response from you.

If you decide to use this study guide in a small-group setting, a good habit is to do some preparation before each meeting. Take some time to read the relevant portions of text and to reflect on the questions and how they apply to you. This will give your group study depth and make the sessions much more fruitful and productive for all.

Because of the personal nature of this study guide, if you use it in a group setting, do remember to keep any sensitive or personal content that is shared within the group. Confidentiality, courtesy, and mutual respect form the foundation for a healthy, safe group. Commit yourself to listening in love to your fellow participants, encouraging one another in the grace of our Lord Jesus and in the revelation of the Scriptures and truths that you are discovering together.

Beloved, whether in personal study or with a group, I am believing with you that you will come away from each session full of hope and faith in the Lord's love for you, and find worry and anxiety gradually losing their grip on your life. May you find yourself learning how to let go of stress and see God's grace flow unabated in the worry-free areas of your life!

I.

LET GO

Your unfulfilled to-do list pulls you in twenty-five different directions with unending demands, responsibilities, and deadlines. You have bills to pay, health issues to attend to, children who need your immediate attention, and endless mountains of emails and text messages that need to be answered. When night comes, it is hard to shut out all your swirling thoughts and worries.

1. We need to hit the Pause button, step back from all the hustle and bustle, and *listen*. What is the most important thing we need to hear?

2. You may have heard of a modern minimalist movement that is all about simplifying and decluttering your surroundings. The premise behind the movement is, if you can tidy up your *outside*, you will find peace on the *inside*. How is the premise of living the let-go life contrary to that?

Letting go of your worries into the hands of the One who created the universe is the most powerful thing you can do. You are acknowledging that you cannot, *but He can*, and you are stepping aside so that His supply can flow into every area of your life. You are making the decision to be still and to let Him be God (see Ps. 46:10), to stand still and to see His salvation (see Ex. 14:13)!

3. Begin to commit to memory 1 Peter 5:7. What is its message of hope for you today and in the future?

4. When Jesus posed the question, "And which of you by worrying can add one hour to his life's span?" (Luke 12:25 AMP), what was He actually telling us?

5. With regard to chronic stress, explain what it means to have life and *life more abundantly* (see John 10:10).

6. Read the story of my meeting with the lady on the plane. What powerful principle was reflected in the lady's release from the fear of flying that will help you to deal with any problem?

Read my vision of the golden pipes coming down from heaven and pouring out golden oil, every pipe bearing constant supply for different areas of the believer's life. This is a key illustration to help you see why letting go of your worries to the Lord is so important.

7. To what areas of a believer's life do the pipes minister?

8. What constricts the flow of the pipe to the believer? What causes the supply to the believer to flow again?

9. What is the basis upon which the heavenly supply can flow into *every* area of our lives?

Our heavenly Father is ever supplying by His grace. He is the God who rained bread from heaven and brought water out from the flinty rock. He is the God who multiplied a little boy's lunch to feed five thousand, with twelve baskets full of leftovers. He is the God who turned water into wine and gave a net-breaking, boat-sinking haul of fishes to a fisherman. There is no problem with the supply! The problem is that we constrict the flow of His supply to the areas we are worried about. We just need to let go to let His supply flow unabated in our lives.

10. What are you discovering about worry and the power of letting go? Write a prayer to the Lord, telling Him how you feel as you reflect on these truths.

11. Read Anita's powerful praise report. What did the Lord keep reminding her to do whenever the bills were due?

12. Belinda's testimony of healing began when she refused to give in to fear and instead held on to God's promises. Why is it untrue to say that you just need to stop worrying and God will supply?

13. The young Christian college student learned he had to L-E-T G-O in order to L-E-T G-O-D. Take a moment to reflect on this. What encouragement does this story give you?

2.

JUST LOOK AT THE BIRDS

Many of us are like the archaeologist in chapter 2's opening story. We hold on to our worries, stress, and anxieties the way he held on to his rope with all his might. We hold on by worrying about our health, our finances, our families, worrying that every worst-case scenario that can happen in our lives will happen. But that's *not* how God wants us to live. He wants us to let go! When we let go and release our worries to Him, He will catch us and uphold us with His everlasting arms of love. As the Bible declares, "Whoever believes in Him [whoever adheres to, trusts in, and relies on Him] will not be disappointed [in his expectations]" (Rom. 10:11 amp).

1. Write out Matthew 6:25 and hear our Lord Jesus speaking the words to you as He did in the Sermon on the Mount.

2. Is your life characterized by *holding on* to your worries or *letting go* of your worries to the Lord? How would you like to live? Talk to the Lord Jesus about it and commit to Him all the worries He is inviting you to let go into His hands.

Jesus continued His Sermon on the Mount, saying, "Look at the birds of the air, for they neither sow nor reap nor gather into barns; yet your heavenly Father feeds them. Are you not of more value than they?" (Matt. 6:26).

3. What lesson do the birds teach us about life? What assurance and hope does this give us?

The devil knows that in the very area you are worried about, that's the area where God's grace doesn't flow. Hence, if the devil can keep you full of worries, he has succeeded in keeping you in a place of defeat. You must understand this: A worried, stressed-out, and anxious believer is a *defeated* believer. That's not the life of faith, victory, abundance, favor, and good success the Lord came to give us.

4. What is the very first thing that the Lord promises to deliver us from in Psalm 91? Explain what it means when you, as a believer, dwell in the secret place of the Most High and abide under the shadow of the Almighty.

5. Scripture teaches us to be good stewards of our finances, to not spend more than we make, to clear our debts, to be generous yet prudent with our money, to have savings and plan for the future. What do the birds teach us about *how* we can do all that?

Jesus taught that we have a heavenly Father who has intimate knowledge of all that we go through and the pressures we face, and that He wants us to release our worries to Him because *He will provide for us*!

6. Jesus said, "*Your* heavenly Father feeds them" (Matt. 6:26, italics mine). Why is this word so beautiful and important? How do you feel knowing this?

Jesus adds, "You are more valuable to God than a whole flock of sparrows" (Matt. 10:31 NLT). If your heavenly Father feeds them and watches over them so carefully, how much more will He provide for you and take care of your practical needs!

7. What is your value according to the Word of God? How much are you worth to God?

8. What assurance does the revelation that God loves you with a personal and in-depth love give you? Take a moment to give thanks to the Lord and share with Him how this blesses you.

9. How did Casey and her husband enter into an abundant supply of God's grace after years of facing lack and extreme stress?

10. How is the revelation that you are immensely loved and valued by your heavenly Father changing deep concerns about your finances, family, or health?

11. If negative experiences, disappointments, and setbacks have conditioned your heart to be less trusting of God's love, how can you start to experience healing?

Let this be the day where you make the decision to let go of your fears to your heavenly Father and trust Him to provide for you!

EXPERIENCE HIS QUALITY LIFE AND HEALTH

Matthew 6:25–34 is one of the most beautiful passages in the entire Bible, spoken by our Lord Himself on the Mount of Beatitudes. If you are struggling to live a carefree, let-go life, I strongly encourage you to take some time to get these words into your heart. They will change your perspective and your life! The power to live the let-go life is in these words spoken from the very mouth of our beautiful Savior. Whatever giants might be before you today, meditate on these words:

> "Therefore I say to you, do not worry about your life, what you will eat or what you will drink; nor about your body, what you will put on. Is not life more than food and the body more than clothing? Look at the birds of the air, for they neither sow nor reap nor gather into barns; yet your heavenly Father feeds them. Are you not of more value than they? Which of you by worrying can add one cubit to his stature?
>
> "So why do you worry about clothing? Consider the lilies of the field, how they grow: they neither toil nor spin; and yet I say to you that even Solomon in all his glory was not arrayed like one of these. Now if God so clothes the grass of the field, which today is, and tomorrow is thrown into the oven, will He not much more clothe you, O you of little faith?
>
> "Therefore do not worry, saying, 'What shall we eat?' or 'What shall we drink?' or 'What shall we wear?' For after all these things the Gentiles seek. For your heavenly Father knows that you need all these things. But seek first the kingdom of God and His righteousness, and all these things shall be added to you. Therefore do not worry about tomorrow, for tomorrow will worry about its own things. Sufficient for the day is its own trouble."

Medical science has demonstrated that stress is cross-generational—young or old, it spares no one. One study showed that 75 percent of Americans reported experiencing at least one symptom of stress in the past month, and this included feeling irritable or angry, anxious, fatigued, depressed, overwhelmed, or having a lack of interest in life. Stress can wreak havoc in your physical body and on your mental health.

1. That same study highlighted the top four sources of stress: Money, work, family responsibilities, and health concerns. What about you? What sources of stress impact you the most?

2. When Jesus asked, "Is not life more than food and the body more than clothing?" what revelation do His words contain?

3. To illustrate how a *quality life* is more than just food, Jesus talked about how God feeds the birds of the air. Explain what He means.

4. To teach us about having a *quality body*, our Lord Jesus tells us how God clothes the lilies and the grass of the field with beauty, glory, and splendor. What did our Lord want us to consider about the lilies of the field? What is He revealing to us about divine health?

The Bible tells us that the grass of the field is alive today, but will be cut and thrown into the furnace as fuel tomorrow. And yet, God clothes them and cares for them. If God even takes care of temporary things that have a transient existence, how much more will He take care of you and clothe you with good health, you who are His cherished and beloved child!

5. Why could our Lord Jesus talk about you receiving His divine health?

6. Write out Ephesians 1:21, Luke 1:37, and Psalm 91:7. Arm yourself with these promises, speak them out loud over every symptom in your body that concerns you, and receive His supernatural peace that will guard your heart and mind.

7. After thirty-eight years of suffering a chronic skin disease, having been seen by over a hundred doctors who told him his condition could not be healed, what finally brought Benson his miraculous healing?

8. Based upon what you have learned in this chapter, take a moment to reflect on how you can start living every day confidently and fearlessly, resting in God's love for you and enjoying the Lord.

4.

THE WAY TO LIVING
WORRY-FREE

When I began my journey of learning to live the let-go life, one of the areas that really got me was my daughter. I did not think I was "worried" about her, but in reality, I was hiding a heart full of laboring over my child's health. And the problem was, the more I was worried about her, the more she seemed to fall ill! In the end, the Lord showed me that my very worrying over her was hindering His supply of health to her.

1. What did the Lord say to me and what did He want me to do?

2. What does the Old English word for "worry" mean? When *you* worry, what does it feel like?

3. We tend to worry about our health, our business, our marriage, or our children. What worries *you*? Has your worrying led to seeing much fruit and supply in the areas you're worried about?

Remember the picture of the golden pipes from heaven that minister God's manifold graces to us? His grace toward us *never* stops flowing. But when we worry about a certain area, it's like we've caught hold of the pipe that brings His supply to that area and we are squeezing it so tightly that His supply cannot flow through to us. Conversely, the Lord showed me that *grace flows in the worry-free areas of our lives*!

4. Because of our Lord's finished work on the cross, what is grace flowing into our lives for, and how can it flow unhindered?

5. In Matthew 6:25, 31–34, our Lord Jesus said the words "Do not worry" three times. Think of all the needs you have. What did Jesus mean when He said that "all these things shall be added to you"?

But Jesus also tells us what is of *first* importance *before* all these things can be added to us—seeking the kingdom of God and His righteousness (see Matt. 6:33).

6. Why is it important to understand His righteousness, and what happens when you do?

7. Spend some time meditating on Romans 5:17. What truth does it convey that defeats the thinking that you have to "get right" with God before you can receive His help in your area of need?

8. As believers in Christ, can we lose our righteousness when we fail? Why or why not? Why is it so important that we know this?

At the cross, the divine exchange took place. As our Lord Jesus became sin with our sin, we became righteous with His righteousness. The Bible declares this: "For He made Him who knew no sin *to be* sin for us, that we might become the righteousness of God in Him" (2 Cor. 5:21). And Romans 5:17 tells us that when we receive the abundance of grace and gift of righteousness, we will *reign in life*!

9. What does it mean to reign in life? Does it require that you be perfect?

10. Write a prayer to the Lord, telling Him how you feel as you reflect on the truth that God sees you righteous based on what Christ has done.

Isaiah 54:14 says, "In righteousness you shall be established; you shall be far from oppression, for you shall not fear; and from terror, for it shall not come near you." "Oppression" is Old Testament language for what we call "stress" today.

11. If you are regularly struggling with stress and fear, what does this verse tell you that you need to do?

12. Read Cali's wonderful praise report. What did she credit as the source of her family's blessings of healing and provision? How can you begin to apply what she did in the areas you're worried about?

13. Jesus said, "Therefore do not worry about tomorrow, for tomorrow will worry about its own things" (Matt. 6:34), because He wants you to enjoy today. Why is it important to live in the present?

5.

THE RHYTHM OF REST

Our heavenly Father desires for us to live a long, good life marked by blessings and health. That is why the closing portion of Psalm 91 says, "With long life I will satisfy him, and show him My salvation" (Ps. 91:16). Long life that satisfies you is your portion in Christ!

1. How would you describe the rhythm of your life today?

2. Beloved, your heavenly Father loves you. You are the apple of His eye and He is *for* you (see Zech. 2:8, Rom. 8:31). What does Isaiah 48:17 (NKJV) tell you about what your Abba Father wants for you?

Quiet yourself by pulling away from all the voices screaming for your attention. Be still and listen to what the Lord is speaking to you through His Word.

Today's frantic rhythm of rushing through life may be all you know. Stress, worry, and anxiety may have inadvertently become a lifestyle, a habit, and maybe even an addiction. God's desire is not for your life to be cut short with stress, but for you to walk in accordance with His rhythm of rest. By the power of the cross, may you be filled with the truth of God's Word, be freed from this oppression of stress, and step into His river of rest.

3. Write out Matthew 11:28–30 (MSG). See how Jesus cares that you are tired, worn out, and burned out. Meditate on how in Him, you can find *real* rest and live freely and lightly.

4. What does "the unforced rhythms of grace" mean?

5. Describe what Jesus means when He says He will give you rest for your *soul*.

6. Jesus' invitation is extended to anyone who is tired and worn out. Are you willing to come? Write a prayer telling Him your response.

7. What does Isaiah 30:15 tell us is the key to strength and long life?

8. What quality of life do Romans 10:11 and Isaiah 28:16 (KJV) say is our portion in Christ?

In Hebrew, one of the words for *rest* is *nuwach*. You find this word appearing in Genesis 8:4 where it says "the ark rested in the seventh month," and in Exodus 20:11 where it says God "rested the seventh day." *Nuwach* is also where Noah's name comes from, so Noah's name means "rest."

9. What divine significance is there in the fact that the first time you find *grace* mentioned in the Bible is in Genesis 6:8, where it says "Noah found grace in the eyes of the LORD"?

10. Why do we want to avoid our bodies' "stress response" or "fight or flight response" being constantly activated by stress?

11. The Hebrew word *nuwach* (rest) originates from the idea of "respiring" or "drawing breath." How does that correspond to deep breathing as one of the ways to quell our bodies' stress response?

Beloved, you don't have to run the rat race like the rest of the world only to become the number one rat. Or focus all your energy to frantically climb the ladder only to realize too late that it was leaning on the wrong building. The Bible tells us that the race is not always to the swift or the battle to the strong, "but time and chance happen to them all" (Eccl. 9:11). The world may depend on toiling to get ahead, but only God can put you at the right place at the right time. You can rest in Him and let Him take your hand and lead you to walk in accordance with His rhythm—the unforced rhythm of grace...and the rhythm of rest!

12. Write down the areas in which you've been pushing yourself to stay ahead out of worry and fear. Ask the Lord to show you how you can apply the unforced rhythm of grace to live the let-go life.

6.

WALKING IN THE RHYTHM OF GRACE

Chapters 4 and 5 of the Gospel of Mark give us a peek into *one* day in the life of our Lord Jesus and an opportunity to watch how He walked in the rhythm of grace. We see how, after spending a whole day teaching the multitudes, He traversed the Sea of Galilee to deliver the most demon-possessed man in the entire Bible, rebuking the windstorm and the waves and calming the water while on the boat. Later, He healed the woman with an issue of blood and raised Jairus' daughter from the dead. All that in *one* day.

1. Based on your reading of the above accounts (see Mark 4:33–5:43), describe what our Lord's rhythm of grace looks like in action.

2. Having read what Jesus did, how do you feel, knowing that our Lord Jesus also hears your cries, is reaching out to you, and wants you to experience His unshakable love and find freedom from any oppression that binds you?

Through Jesus' teaching in John 15:4–5 of Himself as the Vine and we, the branches, the Lord shows us how we can walk with the same rhythm that He walked in. Our Lord Jesus is the true Vine and we are its branches. The Vine and the branches are one. What do the branches need to do? Abide. Simply stay and remain as branches connected to the Vine. We are already there—there isn't any place we are trying to get to. That's how easy the Lord made it for us.

3. What is the only criterion given to us (in John 15:4–5) in order for us to bear fruit? How do we actually practice this on a daily basis?

4. In practical terms, what would your life as a "branch" look like when you are abiding in the Vine?

5. Why does the Lord have to tell us to "*labour* therefore to enter into that rest" (Heb. 4:11 KJV, italics mine) when abiding in the Vine sounds like a simple thing to do?

The only labor that God asks of you is the labor to enter His rest. And as you rest in Him, you will bear *much* fruit in every area of your life! The more you rest and abide in Him, the more His supply flows.

6. Does abiding in Him mean that we become passive and lazy?

7. How does God work in us and through us when we rest?

8. Another way of saying that Jesus is the Vine and we are the branches is found in this truth: "As He is, so are we in this world" (1 John 4:17). Memorize this verse and keep it in your heart. Write a bold declaration of how, as He is healthy, strong, and whole today, so are you. Use it to receive the same health that flows in Him.

Jesus said, "Every branch in Me that does not bear fruit He takes away" (John 15:2). When we study this verse, the phrase "takes away" is actually the Greek word *airo*, which in this context means to "lift up."

9. Why would He lift up the branch in order for it to bear fruit?

10. Throughout the Gospels, we see our Lord Jesus lifting (*airo*) people up, raising to life, restoring. John 15:2 goes on to tell us, "every **branch** that bears fruit He prunes, that it may bear more fruit." What does the Greek word for "prune" mean?

11. Once you have been washed from all your sins by the blood of Jesus, how can you "wash your feet with water" each day?

12. Read Mary and Martha's story in Luke 10:38–42. What "one thing is needed," and what happens when you do that one thing?

Our Lord Jesus Himself prioritized the one thing. Throughout the Gospels, we find Him pulling away from the crowd and going into the wilderness to be with His Father (see Matt. 14:23; Mark 1:35; Luke 5:16, 6:12).

13. Do you want to walk in the restful, unhurried rhythm that our Lord Jesus walked in? How can you learn from Jesus' example and reset your tempo?

7.

REST BRINGS GOD'S COMMANDED BLESSINGS

The Bible tells us that "on the seventh day God had finished his work of creation, so he rested from all his work. And God blessed the seventh day and declared it holy, because it was the day when he rested from all his work of creation" (Gen. 2:2–3 NLT). So we see that the first mention of the Hebrew word for "holy" (*qadash*) is tied up with *rest*.

1. The Creator of the heavens and the earth Himself rested. Do you often tell yourself that you don't need to rest or that you cannot afford to take the time to rest? How do you feel now, knowing that rest is *holy*?

The Sabbath rest was so important to God that He included it in the Ten Commandments (see Ex. 20:8–11). But the Sabbath was already divinely inspired way before the Ten Commandments were given. God rested because He had finished the work (see Ex. 31:17). That was the Rest of Creation.

2. Why does Israel observe the Sabbath on Saturdays, but as believers, our day of rest is on Sunday?

The Jewish Sabbath (or the Shabbat) begins on Friday evening and ends on Saturday evening because the Jewish day *begins* in the evening, which is actually God's way: "So the evening and the morning were the first day" (Gen. 1:5).

    3. What does this show us about how God wants our day to begin?

The first priority in the Jewish observance of the Shabbat is their relationship with God. By resting and setting apart the seventh day, the Jews are acknowledging and remembering that God is the Creator as well as emulating God's example of resting on the seventh day.

    4. How does that correspond to us giving priority to our Sabbath or day of rest?

    5. What is the second priority during Shabbat?

6. Explain why it is so important for you to have kingdom friendships that are replenishing.

7. What does Psalm 92:13 tell us about being a part of a local church if we want to flourish?

8. What did the Harvard University study show is key to keeping us happier and healthier? Take some time to seek the Lord on how you can develop this aspect in your life.

9. What is the third priority of Shabbat, and how does that correspond to why God created man last?

The Scribes and Pharisees had made a whole set of rules and regulations to govern the Sabbath, making it all about dos and don'ts, and forgetting God's original intent: He wanted them to rest. Our Lord Jesus Himself said, "The Sabbath was made for man, and not man for the Sabbath" (Mark 2:27). In other words, God had made the Sabbath for the good of man, not the other way round.

10. Read Colossians 2:16–17. What was the Sabbath instituted to point people to?

11. The religious leaders of Jesus' time were furious that He performed miracles on the Sabbath because they believed He broke the Sabbath law by "working." What did our Lord Jesus show us was the true substance of the Sabbath rest?

12. What encouragement does it give you to know that one touch from Jesus can free you from every shame, stress, and infirmity?

13. Because the children of Israel did not let the land rest every seventh
    year as God had commanded, they were brought into captivity for
    seventy years (see 2 Chron. 36:21). How does this show us that God is
    interested in our good when He tells us to rest?

14. Read the section "Rest Brings Commanded Blessings." What does it
    mean when God says, "I will command My blessing on you" (Lev.
    25:21)?

15. What assurance does His commanded blessings and double-portion
    supply flowing unabated in your life provide to help you let go and
    rest rather than depend on your toiling and laboring?

8.

HAVE A THRONE ATTITUDE

Often, we feel that it is impossible to be at rest when the winds of adversity are blowing full force in our faces. Yet, the Word of God tells us that our Lord prepares a table of provision, healing, and supply for us *in the presence* of our enemies—not *in the absence* of our enemies (see Ps. 23:5). You don't have to wait for all of life's issues to be resolved before you rest. Even now, you can sit back and partake of the feast that He has prepared for you!

1. What enemies are you surrounded by today? How does the promise of Psalm 23:5 encourage you to receive the supernatural peace and rest that our Lord Jesus gives to His beloved?

2. Based on Psalm 110:1 and Ephesians 1:20–23, explain what Jesus' "throne attitude" means. What is the throne attitude we can have and why?

3. In the Old Testament, the priests had to stand ministering daily because their work was never finished. The sacrifices they offered could never take away sins. Why can Jesus, our High Priest, be *seated* at the Father's right hand?

4. Read the second paragraph of the section "We Can Rest in the Presence of Our Enemies." Adapt the words the Father is saying to you beginning with "Sit at My right hand" to whatever you are going through right now and let them bring peace to your heart.

God delivered the children of Israel out of slavery in Egypt and gave them the sure promise that He would bring them into "a land flowing with milk and honey" (Ex. 3:8)—a beautiful picture of God's abundant supply and provision. The fruits in the promised land were pomegranates, grapes, and figs, which hung from vines and trees (see Num. 13:23). The harvesting of the fruits in the promised land was from vines and trees—a picture of how the promises of God are so easy and simple to partake of. The land would have cities that they did not build, houses full of all good things that they did not fill, wells that they did not dig, and vineyards and olive trees that they did not plant (see Deut. 6:10–11). All that is a picture of what God wanted for them—to step into a *finished* work.

5. What empowered Joshua and Caleb to urge the people not to fear but rather to go up at once and take possession of the land?

6. What held the children of Israel back from taking the land, and what was the result?

The children of Israel were not allowed to enter the promised land because they doubted God's Word. However, instead of saying, "They shall not enter My promised land" in the book of Hebrews, God said, "They shall not enter My rest" (Heb. 3:11). God called the promised land "My rest."

7. What is the promised land for believers today?

8. God always tells us to "fear not" (see Isa. 41:10, Luke 12:32), including the giants we face. But what does the Bible tell us *to fear*? How does this encourage you at the same time?

9. Notice that in Kimberly's testimony, she rested in our Lord Jesus before her daughter was restored to her. What revelation does God want you to have in regard to whatever you need Him to do for you?

10. Write out Isaiah 54:1–3 and take a moment to give thanks to the Lord that you can partake of all that Jesus has done on the cross.

11. Even in the midst of your adversity, what do you feel God is personally speaking to your heart that will cause you to break forth into singing and proclaim His praises? In what areas can you start to "enlarge the place of your tent" and "expand to the right and to the left"?

TUNE IN TO PEACE

Read the amazing story of the healing of the woman with the issue of blood and then focus on what our Lord Jesus said to the woman: "Daughter, your faith has made you well. Go in peace, and be healed of your affliction" (Mark 5:34). Our English translation says "go *in* peace," but in the original Greek text the word used is *eis*, meaning "go *into* peace." If "in" had been the intended meaning, the Greek word *en* would have been used. So our Lord wasn't simply bidding her farewell; He was telling her to step *into* the realm of peace, the way you might step *into* a house.

1. What encouragement does the woman reaching out to Jesus and receiving her miracle give you if you're going through a prolonged season of challenges?

2. The peace that the Lord wants us to go into is described in John 14:27. Write out Jesus' words and describe His precious gift to us.

3. What is the difference between the peace Jesus gives and the peace the world gives?

4. Our Lord Jesus did not leave us to fend for ourselves in this world. In John 14:25–26, what did He promise us?

5. The Holy Spirit doesn't only teach us spiritual things. He has been sent to teach us "all things." Explain what that means in practical terms. How does this comfort you when you feel overwhelmed by demands?

6. How does Isaiah 55 instruct us to learn to be led by the Holy Spirit and partake of all that our Lord Jesus did on the cross?

7. Because of the lack of peace, Kenneth chose not to take up an attractive job offer, and soon after his decision he experienced supernatural favor and breakthroughs. Write a prayer to the Lord, asking Him to help you to always be sensitive to His leading and to place you at the right place at the right time.

Right after our Lord tells us that the Holy Spirit will teach us all things, He says, "Peace I leave with you, My peace I give to you; not as the world gives do I give to you. Let not your heart be troubled, neither let it be afraid" (John 14:27).

8. What does this tell us about why it seems as if the Holy Spirit isn't teaching some Christians and leading them to a victorious life?

9. Colossians 3:15 says, "And let the peace of God rule in your hearts." What does the Greek word for "rule" mean and how can that happen for us?

10. Perhaps you've been letting many things—news headlines, bank statements, doctors' reports, or rumors of retrenchment—rule your heart and cause you stress. Practice the let-go life now by saying a prayer of thanks to the Lord for His peace that is already your portion and that is always ready to guard your heart.

Let's go back to the story of the woman with the issue of blood. The Bible tells us that when she touched Jesus' garment, "immediately the fountain of her blood was dried up, and she felt in *her* body that she was healed of the affliction" (Mark 5:27–29). Jesus also told her, "Daughter, your faith has made you well" (Mark 5:34). In other words, she had already been healed.

11. Why then did Jesus still tell her, "Go in peace, and *be healed* of your affliction" (Mark 5:34, italics mine)?

12. What revelation does our Lord Jesus give here in regard to not only receiving healing, but also of walking in divine health? Take a moment to give thanks to the Lord and share with Him how this encourages you.

10.

ALL-ENCOMPASSING *SHALOM*

When our Lord Jesus spoke to His disciples about leaving them His peace in John 14:27, He would have spoken in Hebrew. So the actual Hebrew word Jesus spoke for "peace" was *shalom*. This means He would have told His disciples, "*Shalom,* I leave with you, My *shalom* I give to you." And He would have said to the woman with the issue of blood, "Go into *shalom*."

1. *Shalom* is an all-encompassing word that means much more than just "peace of mind." What is its full meaning?

2. The Bible tells us we can walk in a greater measure of *shalom*: "Grace and peace be multiplied to you in the knowledge of God and of Jesus our Lord" (2 Pet. 1:2)? How is it multiplied—is it through *doing* more?

Once we have the peace *of* God in our hearts, all the inherent benefits of His *shalom*—health, provision, and peace—have been released to us. So the question to ask is not, "Do we have it?" It is already ours! The question to ask is, "Why are we not experiencing more of His *shalom*?"

3. According to John 14:27, how can we keep the *shalom*-peace of God flowing in increasing measures in our lives?

4. Why is it so important for us to not let our hearts be troubled?

5. When confronted with real struggles, sometimes you don't *feel* His peace. In those times, how can you possess your inheritance of peace?

6. So many of Paul's epistles begin with a salutation of grace and peace (see 1 Cor. 1:3, Phil. 1:2, Rom. 1:7). Why do we need both?

7. According to 1 Peter 5:6–8, our enemy, the devil, seeks to steal our peace, because before he can steal anything from us, he must cause us to have troubled hearts. But whom can he *not* devour?

8. What truth about overpowering the devil is stated in Romans 16:20? How do you feel knowing this?

9. The moment a worrisome thought comes to trouble your heart, what two powerful things can you do to remain "undevourable"?

10. Read Rosabel's amazing testimony. What are you learning about staying in peace and confessing verses such as John 14:27?

The Hebrew word *shalom* is tied to the word *shalem*, which means to pay. We cannot have *shalom*—well-being, health, provision, and peace—without a payment. Our Lord Jesus paid the price for our *shalom* by suffering and dying in a horrifying manner on the cross.

11. Why did our Lord allow all that to happen to Him?

12. If you feel you don't deserve peace, health, or forgiveness, you are right. But what gives you a right to it? Reflect on how you can use this truth to guard your heart every time you start feeling agitated with worry or fear.

13. Under the section "How to Be 'Undevourable,'" read the portion about the game the Lord encouraged me to play as He taught me how to walk in His *shalom*-peace in a practical way every day. Try it for yourself. Every time you catch your heart being troubled, say, "Let not your heart be troubled." As you do this, journal the changes that you see in yourself and your situations.

II.

ABOVE ALL THINGS,
GUARD YOUR HEART

To counter stress, many people resort to things such as tobacco, alcohol, or tranquilizers that have harmful side effects and often lead to addictions and other complications. But God's way to counter anxiety and walk in His peace is far better and doesn't have any negative side effects.

1. Philippians 4:6–7 tells us the key by which the peace of God guards our hearts and minds. Compare this passage with Ephesians 6:18. What *is* the key to becoming anxious for nothing and letting God's peace guard your heart, even in the midst of negative circumstances?

The world tries to sell you peace in various forms—breathing techniques, soothing music, calming scents, and time away in solitude. I have nothing against all that. But if having "peace" depends on external circumstances, then it's not true, lasting peace. Peace has to come from inside your heart, and only the Lord Jesus can give you this true peace—a peace that is rugged, strong, abiding, and unaffected by outward circumstances.

2. Peter was imprisoned in a squalid prison, trussed up in two sets of chains and bound to two soldiers, who flanked him at all times. Awaiting trial and the possibility of being executed, one can imagine his fear and desperation. Yet, what does Acts 12:7 tell us?

3. Jesus was unaffected by the tempest on the Sea of Galilee. In fact, He was so full of peace on the inside that He brought peace to His outside circumstances, calming the sea. How can we be the same?

Years ago, the Lord told me something that grew into one of the cornerstone messages of my ministry: *If it's a miracle you need, a miracle you will get—if you remain in peace.*

    4. What was God saying to me…and to you?

Proverbs 4:20–23 tells us to pay attention to the words that will follow because they are *life* to those who find them and *health* to *all* their flesh. Immediately following this instruction, the Bible tells us to *keep our hearts with all diligence.* This means that when we keep our hearts with all diligence, it will bring life to us and health to *all* our flesh.

    5. What does it mean to *keep* our hearts, and why is it so important?

    6. How do you feel when you see Scripture's encouragement to guard only your heart, not everything that isn't going right?

Second Kings tells the powerful story of a Shunammite woman who, when her young son died, did not tell her husband what had happened but that she was going to look for the prophet Elisha. In the midst of this crushing scenario, she simply said, "*It is* well" (2 Kings 4:23, 26). If you study the phrase "*It is* well" with a Hebrew lexicon, you will see that it is made up of only one Hebrew word—*shalom*.

7. Despite this woman's "deep distress" (2 Kings 4:27), what did she keep confessing and declaring, and what did she not say?

8. The Shunammite woman had a robust understanding of *shalom* and was able to guard her heart in the midst of a great trial and adversity by guarding her mouth. What is the correlation between our hearts and our mouths?

9. Whatever situation you might be in, how can you unlock the power of Jesus' *shalom*?

When Jesus rose from the dead and came and stood in the midst of His frightened disciples, the very first words He spoke to them were, "Peace *be* with you," using the word *shalom*. Then He showed them His nail-pierced hands and His pierced side—the receipts of His payment for their *shalom* and the tokens of their guaranteed peace.

10. Why does the enemy try to get us to shut our mouths from speaking forth *shalom* and declaring God's promises?

11. Search out and write down three Scriptures that cover areas troubling you today, and speak those Scriptures over your situations every time you feel fearful!

PEACE IN YOUR CONSCIENCE

We have seen how powerful the peace of God is—how peace on the inside can even change our outward situations, how His *shalom* is all-encompassing and affects every area of our lives, and how our Lord Jesus bequeathed to us His own peace. But until you have a settled peace in your *conscience*, you cannot freely receive what the Lord Jesus has purchased for you.

1. As reflected in what the Lord told me regarding the troubling thoughts I had as a teenager, what do we need to understand to have **settled peace** in our conscience?

2. How did Jesus make it possible for us to have real peace in our conscience?

God loves us. He is *for* us and not against us. He doesn't want us to live under constant condemnation and sin-consciousness, with no confidence that we have been forgiven. There is no peace in such insecurity! He paid the ultimate price to purchase our justification, to give us the gift of no condemnation, to tear down every wall that keeps us from His love.

3. Hebrews 10:10 tells us that we have been sanctified through the offering of the body of Jesus Christ "once for all." How does this give you hope and peace in your conscience when you feel condemned or sin-conscious?

4. Read Romans 8:31–39 slowly, word by word. Let its truths soak into your spirit and silence every bit of insecurity, fear, and doubt you might have in your heart that you can be separated from God's love for you. What assurance and hope does this give you?

5. Based on Romans 5:1–2, what happened the moment you received Christ as your Lord and Savior?

6. Does that mean we don't bother with doing good works? How are these produced when we receive His righteousness as a gift?

7. What truth did Stephie believe that broke her drug addiction?

8. What truth did Jason believe that broke the power of his fears?

9. All we have to do to receive this pure gift of peace is to believe by *faith* in Him who made it possible. How do you feel knowing this?

10. How is an Israelite who applied the blood to his doorposts and then worried all night about his firstborn a picture of many believers? How can we approach concerns for our children or any other area differently?

11. What enabled Abraham to be strong in faith?

12. Why did God send His only begotten Son to be the Lamb who takes away our sins and to bear every punishment and judgment that we deserve?

13. What did Jesus' crown of thorns represent and mean?

He paid the price for our peace of mind. Right now, receive that peace in Jesus' name. Say, "I have peace for my mind. I have the mind of Christ. It has all been paid for and I receive it now in Jesus' name."

14. What remarkable promise are we given in Isaiah 26:3–4?

15. Job 22:21 says that when you are at peace with God, "good will come to you," and 1 Peter 3:10–11 says that if you pursue our Lord Jesus, the Prince of Peace, you will "love life and see good days." How are these and the other powerful truths in this chapter fortifying your heart with a settled peace?

13.

STAND STILL

You can imagine how the children of Israel felt with Pharaoh's army poised to attack on one side and the Red Sea stretched out in front of them like a watery grave. But rather than call the people to take up weapons, Moses said to them, "Do not be afraid. Stand still, and see the salvation of the LORD, which He will accomplish for you today. For the Egyptians whom you see today, you shall see again no more forever. The LORD will fight for you, and you shall hold your peace" (Ex. 14:13–14).

1. What happened when the children of Israel stood still?

2. Miraculously, the Israelites walked "into the midst of the sea on dry *ground*" (Ex. 14:22) and Pharaoh's army was destroyed. What does this tell you about situations where it seems like you have been trapped and there is no way out? How does this strengthen your heart?

You don't have to be afraid of problems in your tomorrows because you have a God who goes before you to lead you and clear the way for you. You don't have to be afraid of attacks coming from behind because the God of Israel is also your rear guard (see Isa 52:12).

3. Even if it looks like there are enemies and challenges coming at you from every direction, why do you not have to fear?

4. The Hebrew word for salvation is *Yeshua*. So what is the Bible saying in Exodus 14:13?

5. The people of the world cry out, "Do something!" When *they* stand still, nothing happens. But what happens and what are we doing when *we* stand still?

6. In the midst of the wilderness, God provided manna and water—not gold and precious stones—when His people hungered and thirsted. What message does this tell us about what He will do for us?

7. In the desert, the Israelites would not have had quail for food or water from a rock had it not been for the Lord. What powerful truth does this tell us about the mind-set God wants us to have?

8. God instructed the Old Testament priests to not gird themselves with *anything that causes sweat.* What do you feel God is speaking to your heart about areas of your life where you are "sweating it"?

9. Write out the powerful declaration that you can speak out every time the enemy demands, "What are you going to do about it?"

10. Why is it significant that Jesus first shed His blood for us from the brow of His head in the garden of Gethsemane (see Luke 22:44)?

11. The root of the Hebrew word "sweat" means "to tremble, quiver, quake, be in terror," or "to agitate (as with fear)," or "vex." Sweat involves agitation and being vexed. The moment the sweat of the Son of God mingled with His blood, what did He redeem us from?

We read in the book of Genesis that the ground in the garden of Eden was cursed (see Gen. 3:17). But when Jesus' blood that redeems fell to the ground in another garden (Gethsemane), the ground was redeemed from the curse for those who believe in Him. Therefore, the ground you step on is redeemed ground, blessed ground, grace ground!

12. Felicia suffered a devastating miscarriage but went on to experience a successful pregnancy and delivery of a baby boy when she looked to the Lord and trusted in Him. Whatever hurts or disappointments we may have experienced in the past, how can we not let them hold us back from putting our trust in the Lord?

13. For whatever you are trusting God for, or dream you are waiting to see happen, what can you start to do today to see your breakthrough come to pass?

14.

BECOMING A
PERSON OF REST

If you have been pushing yourself to the limit, not allowing yourself any respite because of the work that you see ahead of you, the Lord has a word for you in this chapter. He loves you so much. He doesn't want to see you running yourself ragged, thinking that the only way for you to succeed is to work harder and put in more hours. He has a higher way and He has paid the price for you to walk in it.

1. What was the most important factor in God's choice of who would build His house?

2. How does this principle apply to whatever we want to build?

3. What powerful truth regarding rest and letting go does God tell us in Psalm 127:1–2?

4. "Jedidiah," which means "beloved of Jehovah," was the other name of Solomon, whom God chose to build His house. What does it mean for you that "He gives His beloved sleep"?

5. Write out the most basic reason for not missing one night of sleep worrying about your problem, your future, or your life.

6. How does knowing that every good thing in your life comes from God (not man) help you to hold them with a loose hand? What if something doesn't work out as you had hoped?

7. Our church experienced the miracle of successfully tendering for and building the Star Performing Arts Centre when we stayed in God's peace and held all negotiations with a loose hand. Is there an area you need to let go of by doing the same? Commit it to Him right now.

When our church went to secure our first permanent meeting venue, the Lord gave me this beautiful verse that helped me to fight all the battles of anxieties, worries, and cares that I had and to learn to rest in Him: "Sit still, my daughter, until you know how the matter will turn out; for the man will not rest until he has concluded the matter this day" (Ruth 3:18).

8. Read the background of Ruth's story. At the crucial moment when Ruth did not know if Boaz would redeem her, why did Naomi tell her to "sit still"? What was the result?

9. What does it mean to have Jesus as our kinsman Redeemer? How did He redeem us?

10. Read Ruth 3:1. As we stay in His rest, what will the Lord do for us?

Here is a word for those building the local church or serving in a ministry: When David told the prophet Nathan of his desire to build God a house, God was pleased with David's heart for Him. And God told Nathan to tell David, "You want to build Me a house? I will build *you* a house."

11. What assurance does this give you to rest in Him as you commit your ministry to Him or ask Him for fruits in your Christian walk?

12. In chapter 6, we saw how our Lord Jesus could accomplish so much because He rested in His Father, and now He wants you to cast all your cares on Him. What is the relationship between how much you cast your cares to Him and how much He works on your behalf?

Right after Jesus cried out on the cross, "It is finished," He "bowed his head and dismissed his spirit" (John 19:30 TLB). The Greek word for "bowed" is *klino*—the same, seldom-used Greek word for "lay" when He said that the Son of Man has nowhere to "lay" His head (see Matt. 8:20).

13. What did our Lord Jesus finish at the cross for all of us, and in what did He finally find His rest? How does this truth encourage you to let go of the worries you may be carrying today?

14. When Jesus said, "Come unto me...and I will give you rest" (Matt. 11:28 KJV), the original Greek text actually says, "I will rest you." In other words, when you come to Jesus, He Himself will *rest* you. Are you willing to let Him lead you into becoming a person of rest? Write a prayer telling Him your response.

HEAR YOUR WAY
TO VICTORY

Hebrews 4:1–3 tells us it is possible to hear the good news about what our Lord Jesus has done for us on the cross and yet not benefit from it, not be positively changed by it, and not walk in any of the blessings He paid for us to enjoy. This Scripture passage refers to an entire generation of Israelites, who heard the good news that God was bringing them into all of the amazing abundance and provisions of the promised land, and yet failed to enter (see Num. 13:23–26).

1. Why did they fail to enter? What can we learn from this?

2. If you feel that your faith is weak, Romans 10:17 tells us that faith *comes*. How does faith come to us?

3. According to Romans 10:14 and 1 Corinthians 1:21, who brings the word of Christ through which faith comes, and what is the delivery system by which we receive God's blessings?

4. What is God's blueprint for receiving His blessings as expressed in Jesus' ministry?

5. When Solomon asked God for an "understanding" heart, what was he really asking for, and what did he receive?

Our Lord Jesus Himself emphasized the importance of hearing. Over and over again, the Gospels record Him saying, "He who has ears to hear, let him hear!" (see Matt. 11:15, 13:9, 13:43; Mark 4:9; Luke 14:35).

6. What was the "*one thing*" that was needful that Mary chose to do rather than be worried and troubled about *many things* as Martha was?

7. Faith comes by *hearing and hearing* (present continuous tense), not by having *heard* (past tense) as Hebrews 4:2 tells us the children of Israel did. What message does this tell us if we are not *getting* (present continuous tense) healing, blessings, and miracles?

8. In the parable of the sower, what does our Lord Jesus tell us happens *immediately* when we hear the Word of God? Why?

9. What do we fight for in "the good fight of faith" (1 Tim. 6:12)?

10. How does faith defeat anxiety and fear?

11. If you are under attack, fight back with "the sword of the Spirit, which is the word of God" (Eph. 6:17). How do you do that?

If your mind is weighed down by worries and cares, the best thing you can do is to saturate yourself with the Word of God. Keep on hearing and hearing. With modern technology—audiobooks, mobile apps, and online streaming—you can be washed by the water of the Word anywhere and at any time of the day. As you listen to Christ-filled sermons, you will be filled with hope, charged with audacious faith, and greatly strengthened by His love!

12. Settle it in your heart that *one thing* is needful—prioritizing your time with Him. As we take time to wait on Him, what amazing promise are we given in Isaiah 40:31?

With an understanding of the Greek tenses used, you can read Galatians 3:2, 5 this way: "He who is *constantly supplying* you the Holy Spirit and *constantly working* miracles among you, does He do it by the works of the law, or by the hearing of faith?" It may seem simple, but God works miracles by the hearing of faith. God is constantly supplying us with miracles. Our part is to let go, listen to His Word, and let His supply flow.

13. Paul and Barnabas were preaching *the gospel* in Lystra (see Acts 14:7), and the crippled man who had never walked *heard* Paul speaking. Explain what "heard" here means and what it led to.

14. What message was Paul and Barnabas preaching?

15. Perhaps you are in a situation that looks impossible or grappling with a dire medical diagnosis like cancer as Leah shared in my book. Take a moment to reflect on how you can start hearing your way to faith and victory. Ask the Lord to help you develop this important spiritual discipline.

THE ONE THING THAT BRINGS SUCCESS IN EVERY AREA

Listening to the Word is so important, but don't stop there. As you hear, get hold of what speaks to you, meditate on it, and make it yours. Look for God's faith images in His eternal, everlasting, and unshakable Word that will establish and stabilize your heart against all the negative images the world presents to suffocate your heart with fear.

1. On another sheet of paper, write or print out Psalm 1:1–3 and place it where you will see it every day. Commit it to memory and repeat it out loud every morning. What does it mean that you are like a tree *planted* by the *rivers* of water?

2. What does it mean to bring forth fruit in season?

3. What does the passage also say about your success?

Psalm 1:2 tells us that the key to being the blessed man is "his delight *is* in the law of the LORD, and in His law he meditates day and night."

4. Explain what it means to *delight* in the Word of the Lord. Reflect on how meditating on the Word can also be a delight to you.

5. What message does the Hebrew word for *meditate* hold for us?

6. What is Joshua told to do to make his way prosperous and full of good success? How does this apply to you if you want the same?

7. True prosperity is *holistic* (it is not only about money). Explain what that means. Similarly, what does *good* success in all areas of your life imply?

Many are meditating on their worries, troubles, and challenges day and night. Our heavenly Father is showing us how to live the let-go life by letting go of our worries and replacing them with His Word, so we will be like the fresh and flourishing tree described in Psalm 1!

8. How is meditation very much like the process of rumination?

9. What are some ways you can start to meditate on God's Word?

10. Closely study the section where I show you how to meditate on just one verse, specifically Romans 8:32. Then on a separate sheet of paper, in a similar manner, write down your meditations for the one verse, "The Lord is my Shepherd [to feed, guide, and shield me], I shall not lack" (Ps. 23:1 AMPC). Don't rush through it. Break it into individual words and phrases and take your time to meditate on each, turning them around to allow every truth in them to speak to your heart and nourish you.

11. What does 1 Timothy 4:15–16 say about meditation?

12. What powerful principles are reflected in Paula's praise report that
     will help you to keep feeding and feeding on God's truths? What
     encouragement do you draw from this?

I encourage you to listen to sermons and read God's Word whenever you can as well as take some time each day to really meditate on the verses that you hear or read. You can start with just one verse a day. It's not about how many chapters you read, but the depths that you plunge into, and how deeply you go to really digest and think about the words that the Holy Spirit chose, and why He phrased it the way He did. Take time to ruminate on the Word, chewing it and savoring it until the essence of one verse becomes such a truth it drowns out the facts that could be staring you in the face.

13. **Whatever is troubling you now, find Scriptures that speak to that situation, write them down, meditate on them, and speak forth the truth of God as a powerful declaration of victory.**

May you become like the blessed man planted by the rivers of water, always bringing forth fruit in season. Even in seasons of heat, may you be at rest and full of strength and life, and may whatever you do prosper in the mighty name of Jesus. Amen!

17.

EXPERIENCING BLESSINGS IN MARRIAGE

If you're married but you and your spouse are constantly quarreling and getting upset with each other, it is hard to live the let-go life. That's why in this chapter, I want you to look with me at God's heart for your marriage and how you can invite the Lord Jesus into your marriage so that you can live the victorious, let-go life as a couple. Don't try to deal with all your stress and anxieties on your own—learn to live the let-go life together.

1. What are some practical ways in which you and your spouse can practice living the let-go life?

2. Together, what amazing power do you and your spouse hold? What is the secret to strengthening this power?

3. What does it mean to "hearken diligently" to God's Word, and what is promised to us when we do?

The key to having a marriage that is full of love and affirmation, instead of strife and contention, is to keep on listening to His Word together!

4. Why does the enemy work so hard to make marriages fail?

Whatever the attack on your marriage, know that God loves you and cares about your marriage. Your marriage is important to Him.

5. No matter what challenges you are facing in your marriage, how do you feel knowing that God by His grace and practical supply can move you toward "days of heaven upon the earth"?

Marriage was God's first priority. Long before God ordained a church, God ordained the institution of marriage in the garden of Eden. The very first miracle Jesus performed and that started His ministry was at a wedding. God's heart is for your marriage and His Word is so full of truths about His supernatural supply in this area. He will cause you to step into a whole new level of intimacy in your marriage.

6. Every marriage experiences valleys. Like the wine at the wedding in Cana, human love can run out. How does this happen? In what ways can you identify with this?

7. Read Ecclesiastes 4:12. What "third party" does every marriage need in order to thrive?

8. Why will you be disappointed whenever you put your spouse in a place where all your happiness depends on him or her? How can you avoid this trap?

When Jesus turned the water into wine, He compressed what typically took years to produce and in an instant produced the highest quality wine. He can do in a short time what takes years through human effort. One moment of His favor can turn your whole marriage around.

9. What does Joel 2:25 promise that God can do in your marriage?

10. The consequences of adultery are devastating and far-reaching. When King David committed adultery with Bathsheba, God sent him a message through Nathan. What can we learn from God's message to David if we are not satisfied with our marriages?

11. What should we always be asking the Lord for in our marriages?

12. Even if you have failed, how can the Lord still bless and restore your marriage?

13. Every challenge that you can face in your marriage has been borne by your Savior at the cross. What is your part?

14. Describe the supernaturally natural way the Lord restored the marriage of the couple who came to our church in Singapore.

15. Whatever issues you are facing in your marriage today, let go of your regrets, anger, or fears to the Lord and cast your concerns to Him. Whatever the state of your marriage, ask Him for more of His grace to heal and strengthen your marriage.

As you let go and rest in Jesus' finished work, instead of all your efforts, I am believing with you that His miracle-working power will begin to flow and you will see Him do a new thing in your marriage!

18.

STRESS-FREE PARENTING

The stress of parenting is very real. Making the decision to let our hearts not be troubled when it comes to our own lives is already difficult—how much more mammoth of a feat it is when it involves our kids! God desires for us to experience *days of heaven upon the earth* and this speaks of blessings over our households, our marriages, as well as our children. Just as you want to see your children successful, stress-free, healthy, and flourishing in the house of God, how much more does our Father in heaven desire that for them!

1. Take a moment to reflect on the amazing promise in Deuteronomy 11:18–21 that God wants to give us and our children long life, as well as days that are "as the days of heaven upon the earth." What does He tell us to prioritize as parents?

2. How does God want us to teach our children about His words?

3. In Deuteronomy 11:19, what is the Hebrew word left untranslated that tells us *what* we should speak to our children about?

4. To help you make Jesus a part of your everyday life with your children, I provided some practical ways you can do that in your daily settings. Create your own list of what you think will work for you and your children.

Every child is different and the Holy Spirit will show you what works for your children.

5. As you keep speaking of the Lord Jesus, praying over your children, meditating on the Word in front of your children, sharing testimonies of breakthroughs with them, and playing anointed psalms, hymns, and worship songs or sermons in the background at home, what are you doing? Why is this important?

6. Why should you not be discouraged even if your children don't look like they are interested in God's Word?

7. As was shown through Joscelin's testimony, no matter what challenges your children are going through, what is the most crucial thing you can do for them?

8. Jochebed hid baby Moses "by faith." How are we to deal with negative reports "experts" give us about our children that can cause stress?

9. Jochebed put baby Moses into an "ark." What is that a powerful picture of, and how does it apply to us as parents?

10. As can be seen from Jochebed's story, what can happen to our children when we put them in the Lord's hands and trust Him?

11. Whatever your children may be going through, what promise from Isaiah 54:13 can you stand upon?

12. Our children can walk in this great *shalom* because Isaiah 54 and its promises come after Isaiah 53, which is all about the work of our Lord Jesus at the cross. Take some time to meditate on Isaiah 53. Then write your declarations of what our Lord Jesus has done for your children so that you can let go and place them in His care.

19.

LET GO AND LIVE LONG

This chapter is all about God's desire for you to live a long, healthy life, a let-go life free to fully enjoy the blessings that He has prepared for you. The eternal Word of the living God declares that with *long life*, He shall satisfy you (see Ps. 91:16). I believe the Lord has hidden secrets to health in His Word that will bless you, especially when you see how it is all linked to what we have been talking about throughout this book.

1. What does the Hebrew word for "sound," describing the heart in Proverbs 14:30 (NKJV), tell you?

2. If you remove the first Hebrew letter from the word *marpe* to get to its root, you get the word *rapha*. What does *rapha* mean, and how does it relate to the act of relaxing?

3. When you put together the corresponding picture or idea for each Hebrew letter of the word *rapha*, what do you see?

4. Write out Proverbs 4:20–22. Take some time to meditate on and memorize this powerful verse of Scripture.

5. What does God tell us to do with His words and sayings? When we do that, what will His words do?

6. If we receive a negative medical report, what encouragement does 2 Corinthians 4:18 give us?

7. Even when the symptoms of the disease remained, Dana and her husband kept believing, meditating on, and declaring God's Word, and healing came. What can you learn from their experience?

8. God desires to give you a long, fulfilling, and healthy life. Why do you not need to accept deterioration as you grow older?

9. How do Caleb, Moses, and Sarah demonstrate that your youth can be renewed like the eagle's (see Ps. 103:5)?

10. After heroically serving the Lord into his nineties with ease, George Müller died with no aches or pains. What did he say was one of his secrets to long life?

11. Müller lived a long, significant life and was used mightily by God because he truly lived a let-go life. How did he live in the reality of Philippians 4:6–7, which we discussed in chapter 11 of the book?

12. What does Deuteronomy 30:19–20 tell us is God's supernatural prescription for long life?

13. How does Psalm 91:16—"With long life I will satisfy him, and show him My salvation"—also contain the secret of long life?

14. Long life is connected to seeing Jesus in the Word of God, because when we do, we partake of His resurrection life and divine health. Write a prayer asking Him to show you more and more of Himself and His grace in the Word. If you are trusting Him for healing, take time also to write down what He is showing you about Himself as your healer and the power of His finished work.

20.
YOU ARE NOT ALONE

Don't be too hard on yourself when you find yourself bogged down with worries and your heart loaded with anxieties even after learning about the let-go life that God wants you to live. Living the let-go life is a daily journey of faith. Every day, there is a battle for our minds. New issues can arise and we can find ourselves faced with multiple challenges coming at us from different fronts. You can choose to allow your mind to stress out over all the possible worst-case scenarios and hold on to your cares with as much strength as you can muster. Or you can choose to step into the river of faith and start practicing the let-go life.

1. What marvelous assurance does Psalm 61:2–4 provide?

2. How do you feel knowing that God knows all your cares and secret struggles and questions, and wants to be your strong tower, shelter, and refuge?

During one of the darkest periods in Israel's history, God used the prophet Elijah in a mighty way to repeatedly demonstrate that He alone is God and that Baal was powerless. Read the story of Elijah's confrontation with the prophets of Baal, the wicked King Ahab, and the evil Queen Jezebel in chapter 20 and in 1 Kings 16–19. We see how Elijah called down fire from heaven, how the prophets of Baal were destroyed, and how God gave Elijah a resounding victory.

3. The Bible also tells us Elijah was a man with a nature like ours, with the same physical, mental, and spiritual limitations and shortcomings. So what caused Elijah to run for his life, despite everything God had done through him, when threatened by Jezebel?

4. What did Elijah forget?

5. Beyond his fear, what did Elijah end up feeling?

In just one moment, any of us can lose sight of a good God. Even if we walked in the greatest faith yesterday, we can go back to sight today.

Like Elijah, for a wide variety of reasons, many believers suffer depression and discouragement, and perhaps feel disappointed with God. I want you to see what God did for Elijah because I believe that it will lift you out of the darkness that has surrounded you.

6. Who was "the angel of the LORD" (1 Kings 19:7) who came to Elijah? What did He do for Elijah, and what does He do for us when we are discouraged?

7. For forty days and forty nights, Elijah went on the strength of the food the angel of the Lord had given him. What food does He give us today?

8. Notice also that God gave Elijah sleep. How do you feel, knowing that God cares for you so intimately and practically?

In the day of Elijah's faith, ravens fed him and the widow sustained him. But in the day of his depression, angels waited on him, and God Himself fed him. What a God! His mercies fail not. They are new every morning!

9. Rather than forsake us in our day of depression, what does God do for us? What is His message for us?

10. Elijah got discouraged because He thought that God had left him all alone in his battles, yet God showed him it wasn't true. When you feel isolated and think God doesn't care, what is the Lord encouraging you to do?

11. We often look for spectacular signs to tell us that God is with us. Read 1 Kings 19:11–12. Elijah had a powerful encounter with the Lord, but through what did the Lord actually get His message to Elijah? How is He speaking to you and assuring you today?

David wrote these lines in a beautiful psalm: "My heart has heard you say, 'Come and talk with me.' And my heart responds, "Lord, I am coming" (Ps. 27:8 NLT). The Lord is the still, small voice that is whispering to you right now, "Come and talk with Me." He is saying, "Come to Me, all *you* who labor and are heavy laden, and I will give you rest" (Matt. 11:28). Come to Him with all your hurts, your disappointments, and your failures. He wants to give you His rest. He wants to give you His peace.

12. Read the beautiful words of the hymn, *Tell It to Jesus*. Take some time to write out whatever is on your heart and cast it into His loving care, knowing He will not rest until He resolves the matter for you (see Ruth 3:18).

As you come to the close of this study guide, I pray you've encountered our Lord Jesus in a deep and intimate way. Remember, when worry and fear come knocking, when you get discouraged, tell it to Jesus. He is your loving Savior and friend who sticks closer than a brother, and He is more than willing and able to handle your problems and save you. As you learn to cast your cares to Him every day, may you begin to live the let-go life, free from fear, stress, and anxiety!

CLOSING WORDS

Throughout this study guide, it has been my privilege to share with you what the Lord has revealed to me through the years about living a life free from crippling cares, anxieties, and stress by depending on His love and grace. It's my prayer that as you have taken this wonderful journey with me, you have begun to experience a deeper inward rest and *shalom*-peace grounded on God's unshakable Word.

We live in a world where we're surrounded by fears, uncertainties, responsibilities, and demands 24/7. This is why it's so important for us to be established in how God's grace is all about supply. When you feel the chokehold of a demand mind-set starting to claim your heart, remember the picture of the golden pipes constantly bringing fresh supply from heaven into every area of need. Remember that as you practice letting go of your worries by casting them into His hands and letting His promises anchor your heart, you're relaxing your grip and allowing His supply to flow.

Beloved, you are of immense value to the Father, who gave up His Son, heaven's darling, for you. His love for you didn't end there, but is still giving to, healing, and delivering you in all the practical ways you need Him to. I pray that as you learn to stand still and let Him fight your battles, you will begin to enjoy days of heaven upon the earth and walk in new levels of victory!

ANSWERS

CHAPTER 1

1. Most importantly, we need to pause and listen to the everlasting words of the One who loves us. This is not about reading another book. This is about being refreshed. This is about taking a cool evening walk with our Lord. This is about hearing Him whisper to us, "Be still, and know that I *am* God" (Ps. 46:10).

2. The premise of this book is, if you can declutter what is *inside* you—in your heart, your soul, and your mind—the clutter that is on the *outside* will be taken care of. The Spirit of the Lord works from the inside out. Yes, you might be faced with a mountain of demands, but when there is a song in your heart, any mountain can be surmounted. Take care of the knots on the inside, and the knots on the outside will be supernaturally untied.

3. You can cast *all* your cares on Him *once and for all* because He cares for you. It doesn't matter what you are anxious about. Whether you fear becoming irrelevant in the marketplace, or are stressed about the upcoming interview, or are worried you might end up unloved and alone, you can take that care and put it in His hands. Your Father loves you with the deepest affection and watches over you so carefully. He is waiting for you to let Him take over.

4. Our Lord was telling us *not* to hold on to our worries because all our worries and anxieties cannot change any situation. No amount of worrying on our part can cause us to live even a little longer. In fact, worry and stress can be detrimental to us and shorten our lives!

5. God doesn't want us to just have a trickle of life or just enough life. He wants us to have overflowing life! Being bowed down with cares, fighting chronic fatigue, or battling stress and sickness is not living life more abundantly. Our Lord Jesus loves you so much and He wants you to cast *all* your cares to Him because He does not want you to live a life of worry, but a life of abundant peace, health, and strength!

6. No matter how tightly we clutch and hold on to our problems, all our holding on is not going to keep the plane up in the air, so to speak. When it comes to Jesus, you can let go, trust His piloting, and enjoy the journey.

7. In my vision, one of the golden pipes ministered to the believer's health, another pipe ministered to his finances, while yet another ministered to his marital well-being. Another pipe ministered to his walk with God, with *charismata*, anointings, and spiritual gifts flowing down from heaven. Another golden pipe ministered to his sense of peace.

8. Getting worried about a particular area of his life constricts the pipe on his end. All he has to do is to stop worrying and let go…and the supply will flow out again.

9. When our Lord Jesus died on the cross, He paid for our healing, for our provision, for our peace, for our marriages to be blessed, and for the well-being of our children. He paid for golden pipes filled with golden oil to flow unabated over us, bringing supply constantly into our lives.

11. The Lord kept telling her, "Take no thought for tomorrow, My grace is sufficient for you." She chose not to worry about how she would provide for her family and believed that all things would work together for her good. God gave her "significantly more" than what she asked for!

12. Because the truth is that God *has* already supplied and He is *still* supplying. Your worrying is hindering your receiving, so let go.

13. In the midst of your worries, let go and let God be God in your life. Let go and allow His abundant supplies of health, strength, victory, peace, provision, and so much more to flood your life.

CHAPTER 2

1. "Therefore I say to you, do not worry about your life, what you will eat or what you will drink; nor about your body, what you will put on. Is not life more than food and the body more than clothing?"

3. Birds show us the carefree life that God intends for us to live. They don't sow nor reap, nor gather into barns, and yet our heavenly Father feeds them. He provides even for the birds—how much more will He provide for you, oh child of God!

4. He promises to deliver us from the snare of the fowler! In the secret place of the Most High, the Word of God promises you that God Himself will *surely* (not maybe) deliver you from the snare of the fowler—from all stress, all worries, and all anxieties. What an awesome place to live in! What a great way to live the carefree, let-go life. In that place, you can live like a bird that soars freely in the sky, not like a bird trapped in the snare of the fowler!

5. The birds teach us that we can do all of these things *without* stress! God wants us to have a career but not be stressed by it. Our supply does not come only from our jobs; our heavenly Father who feeds the birds of the air is our source and our supply!

6. For the Jewish people, the idea of God being their *Father* (or in their vernacular, *Abba*) was a very foreign concept. They knew God as *Elohim*—the all-powerful being—and not as a loving, affectionate, and caring Father. But Jesus came to reveal the name *Father* to the people! He came to show us that God is not just a powerful God, but also a *Father* who loves us dearly. He's our Papa, our Daddy, our Abba (see Rom. 8:15). Our Lord was unveiling to the people then and to us today that we have a heavenly Father who cares even about feeding common birds.

7. What was the price He was willing to pay to purchase your forgiveness and your salvation (which includes your health, your peace, your wholeness, and your mental soundness)? The Bible tells us that God did not spare His own Son. He gave His own Son up for *you* (see Rom. 8:32)! Our Lord Jesus was God's only begotten Son, the Son whom He loved, the Son who was daily His delight (see Prov. 8:30). And yet, God loved *you* so much that He gave His Son up for you (see John 3:16). God paid for your redemption with the blood of His Son. That is how much God values and loves you!

8. God's love is not general. And neither is He only involved in the "big things" of life. His love for you is intricately detailed and He is intensely involved in the day-to-day minutiae of your life. He cares about every detail of your life.

9. God's supply began to flow unhindered in their financial situation when they began to live the let-go life and release to God what Casey described as "extreme stress." The more they received an abundant supply of His grace— His unmerited, unearned, and undeserved favor—by hearing and hearing the preaching of the gospel of grace, the more they made the shift from extreme stress to His rest. And in that rest, God's supply of provision flowed unhindered without their stress and worries.

10. When you know how much God loves and values you, you will never again fear that your needs will not be provided for. You will never again be worried about your health or stressed about your future or the well-being of your children. You can stop holding on and start living the relaxed, carefree, let-go life!

11. Release the wounds, hurts, and bitterness of the past into His loving hands. Your heavenly Father is not the author of your pain. He is the author and finisher of your amazing future in this life (see Jer. 29:11). He values you so much He sent His own Son to ransom and redeem you.

CHAPTER 3

2. Our Lord Jesus was speaking to us about experiencing a quality life and having quality health for our bodies. He is saying that a quality body is more important than the clothes you wear, and a quality life is more important than the food you eat. Remember, Jesus came to give us life and life more abundantly!

3. When God gives us a quality life, there *will* be food! We can have a quality life because we have a heavenly Father who values us and will take care of all our practical needs. When you love someone, as an earthly father does his children, your great joy is to see them free from worries. Imagine how much more our Abba wants to see us completely without worry? Our part, even as we manage our jobs and various responsibilities, is to live freely and without cares because *He* is our provider!

4. Flowers do not grow physically healthy and strong by toiling and spinning. *Your* heavenly Father clothes them! With all his wealth, Solomon could buy the most exquisite clothing, but he could not buy what the lilies had—health. Money can buy you access to the best doctors and medical facilities, but it can't buy you health. Divine health comes only from the Lord! He clothes you with the best clothing—divine and supernatural health—that one could have. And you don't even have to toil or spin because it is a *gift* that you can simply receive because of what Christ has done! Hallelujah!

Divine health doesn't come from spending hours working out or dieting.

You can get fit naturally, but divine health—the quality of health that clothed the lilies—comes from the Lord. So by all means, hit the gym, lift, run, brisk walk, and eat wisely—just do it without being stressed out over the condition of your body. Let go of the fears about your physical body and let the Lord supply to you His abundant and quality life, as well as His divine health and resurrection power.

5. Because He knew that He would be paying for it for us. He knew what He was going to go through at the cross for you and me. He knew that He would be purchasing for us health, wholeness, and strength with His own body. Today, we live on the other side of the cross. He has already paid the price so that right now, you can declare that by His stripes, you *are healed* (see Isa. 53:5). You are not *going to be* healed; you are *already* healed in Christ!

6. Our Lord Jesus is "far above all principality and power and might and dominion, and every name that is named, not only in this age but also in that which is to come" (Eph.1:21). "For with God nothing will be impossible" (Luke 1:37). "A thousand may fall at your side, and ten thousand at your right hand; *but* it shall not come near you" (Ps. 91:7).

7. Benson said, "I started to believe that God blesses those whom He loves, and started to *rest in what He has done for me* and not trust in what I was trying to do for Him….Pastor Prince shared about the Lord's restoration in some of his messages, and I have been restored. My new skin is the least of the blessings. God has also restored to me His perfect peace. *I no longer worry, but I just cast my cares on Him and receive His favor. Fear and oppression are far from me.* Thank You, Jesus, for going to the cross for me."

CHAPTER 4

1. The Lord said, "Cast your daughter into My hands and I will take care of her. I love her more than you can. And the best attitude you can have toward your daughter is to be carefree. Don't worry about her anymore."

2. The word *worry* comes from the Old English word *wyrgan*, which means "to strangle." And sometimes it feels like that. When you worry, it feels like you're being strangled of the very life, of the very breath, you're breathing.

3. I submit to you that you are not seeing much fruit or supply in the area you're worried about precisely because you have been worrying instead of putting the problem in the Lord's hands and allowing His grace to flow.

4. Grace is flowing for our health, for the soundness of our minds, and for our intimacy with the Lord. Grace is flowing for us to walk holy, for us to have revelation of His Word, and for us to have the wisdom to parent our children. His grace is flowing and as long as you *refuse to let your heart be troubled*, the grace of God flows unhindered to you in every area.

5. Jesus said that all the things we need shall be "added," not just "given." One can give only the bare minimum, but "added" speaks of ever increasing. In other words, *all* these things shall be added to you in greater quantity and quality (see Eph. 3:20)! And He cares for you even beyond basic concerns. In the last chapter, we saw how our Lord Jesus wants us to enjoy quality lives and have quality bodies. *All* these things shall be added to you!

6. Unless you are *first* established on the foundational truth that you are righteous because of what Jesus has done, you will not be able to let go and let His supply flow into your life. Knowing that you are righteous in Christ is what gives you the confident assurance to let go of your cares, worries, and anxieties to the Lord. So your first priority each day is to seek *His* righteousness, and "all these things"—whether it is food, clothing, or other necessities in life—will be added to you. They will not just be given to you, but *added* to you as your inheritance in Christ. You don't need to use your faith for every single need in life. You just need to use your faith for one thing—to believe that as a child of God, you are the righteousness of God in Christ (see 2 Cor. 5:21)—and it will cause all the blessings you seek to come after you and overtake you!

7. When you received Jesus Christ as your Lord and Savior, you received the gift of righteousness. We did not become righteous by *doing good*; we received righteousness as a *gift*. And because we have the gift of righteousness, all the good things that Jesus deserves, we get (see Eph. 1:3).

8. As believers in Christ we *cannot* lose our righteousness *even when we fail*. In fact, it is His righteousness that can help us up when we fail! This is so important for you to know because like it or not, you *will* fail. You *will* fall short. And if you are not established in your righteousness in Christ, the devil will accuse you and make you think that you don't deserve to be healed, that you are not qualified to receive His supply, and that you should be condemned to live a defeated life filled with stress, worries, and anxieties.

9. To reign in life means you have the power to win over every sin and addiction, to break free from the bondage of the enemy and walk in greater measures of victory and holiness! The good news is, you can trust God for healing and provision not because everything in your life is perfect, but because of His righteousness in your life. God does not move for you because you are perfect in every way. He moves on your behalf because of what our Lord Jesus has accomplished at the cross. The more you understand His righteousness, the less you will struggle to let go of your cares to Him.

11. When you are established in His righteousness, you are far from stress because you are not fearful. If you find it extremely challenging to let go of your worries and anxieties to the Lord, perhaps you are not truly established in His gift of righteousness and you are still depending on your own righteousness. Keep listening to the gospel of grace until this truth is cemented in your heart and you know beyond the shadow of a doubt that all the blessings of the righteous belong to you. May you be so assured that because you are righteous, your prayers avail much (see James 5:16) and you can cast all your cares to the Lord!

12. The belief that she and her family are righteous by faith in Jesus' finished work on the cross.

13. When He gave *manna* to the children of Israel, He gave it to them *daily* (see Ex. 16:4). He doesn't give you tomorrow's bread today. He only gives you sufficient supply for *today*. Don't try to live next week today. There is no supply and grace for next week today. There is only grace for today. When tomorrow comes, He wants you to look to Him again for the supply. In other words, the Lord wants you to live one day at a time.

CHAPTER 5

2. Your Abba wants to guide you on how to live life because He loves *you*. He wants you to profit in your marriage and family life, your financial life, your social life, and your health. He wants to see you succeed in every area of your life and He wants to lead you by the way you should go.

3. "Are you tired? Worn out? Burned out on religion? Come to me. Get away with me and you'll recover your life. I'll show you how to take a real rest. Walk with me and work with me—watch how I do it. Learn the unforced rhythms of grace. I won't lay anything heavy or ill-fitting on you. Keep company with me and you'll learn to live freely and lightly."

4. Our Lord Jesus has a rhythm. Grace has a rhythm. It is unforced, gentle, easy, and light for those who keep company with our Lord Jesus.

5. This means that in Christ, there is rest for your worried *mind*, for your turbulent *emotions*, and for your troubled *heart* and *conscience*—a rest that goes down deep into your spirit. Walk with Him. Keep company with Him and He will show you how to take a *real* rest. His rest is not just a physical rest even though that is important. The rest that He gives you will refresh you and strengthen you.

7. It says that in returning to God and resting in Him, you will be saved. In quietness and confidence (in God) shall be your strength. The Hebrew word for *strength* here is the same word used in Psalm 90:10 when it talks about the strength to live a long life. This tell us that the more at rest you are, the more it will *prolong your life!*

8. Whoever believes in God can be steady, calm, and cool; he does not have to make haste. I believe the Lord is telling us, "Slow down." Maybe the people of the world have to be hasty because they can only rely on themselves to watch their backs. But you have a heavenly Father. Don't keep striving, rushing, and pushing to get ahead. In Christ, we are in this world but not *of* this world. The rhythm of the world is forceful, aggressive, and hurried. But we are called to walk in the unforced rhythms of grace!

9. Every time the Bible mentions something for the first time, there is a divine significance. In this case, it is saying that *rest finds grace with the Lord.* When you are in rest, you will find grace with the Lord. Grace means you are not working; God is working. When we rest in Him, we find Him working on our behalf!

10. Because it leads to an over-release of cortisol and other stress hormones. This puts us at risk of many health problems, including anxiety, depression, digestive problems, headaches, heart disease, sleep problems, weight gain, and memory and concentration impairment. The stress response also suppresses the immune system, increasing our susceptibility to colds and other illnesses.

11. Deep breathing is one of the ways by which we can lower cortisol levels in our bodies. The original idea for *nuwach* (rest) lies in drawing breath. One of the natural means to being at rest was hidden for us in the Hebrew word *rest!* Let everything that has breath praise the Lord!

CHAPTER 6

1. Jesus accomplished so much, yet He was always restful, never hurried. He was not frazzled by the multitude that thronged Him or burdened by the incessant demands placed on Him. Whether it was for the lowly woman whom others considered unclean or for the stately ruler of the synagogue, our Lord Jesus always had time.

3. Our part is to abide in Christ. Our part is to rest! As we abide in Him and put our trust in Him, we *will* bear fruit because of the supply of sap, life, and fatness that flows to us from the Vine. In fact, the supply is constantly flowing (remember my vision of the golden oil flowing through the golden pipes?) and the branches simply have to remain as branches and not restrict the supply.

4. When you are faced with a stressful situation, your Vine—our Lord Jesus—supplies you with His peace. When you need to make a key decision and you don't know what to do, your Vine supplies His wisdom. When you have to tackle many tasks but feel so tired, His strength flows through you. What a life of rest that is!

5. It is so hard for us to rest because we want to have a part to play. We want to do something. We want to get some of the glory. Other times, it's because of unbelief—we find it so hard to believe that God has done it all. That is why the only labor that God tells us to pay attention to is the labor to enter His rest.

6. Abiding in Him and living the life of rest is not about living a passive, lazy life. I'm not talking about sitting on your hands and doing absolutely nothing. When you are connected with Him, there will be a divine supply of life and rhythm that is not frantic. You will be doing things by the leading of the Holy Spirit, yet not exhausted because you're not depending on your own efforts and driven by fear. You will be like the burning bush, burning strong but not burning out. There will be fruits and divine results when you're trusting God and depending on His leading and supply. This is very different from simply doing nothing out of laziness or passivity. Just look at our Lord Jesus Christ. No one was more active yet restful than He was.

7. As new covenant believers, we live by grace, which is about *resting* in the power of the Holy Spirit, who works in us to give us both the willingness and the ability to do what pleases God (see Phil. 2:13). God gives us the desires to do what He wants us to do, and then He gives us the power to perform it.

9. If the branch is lying in the dust on the ground instead of being lifted up on a trellis, it cannot bear fruit. In the same way, the reason many believers cannot bear fruit is that the devil has cast them down and they are stressed out and depressed—they are wallowing in the dust.

10. The Greek word used for "prune" here is *kathairo*, which means "to cleanse." The vinedressers in Jesus' time used to pour water on the branches to cleanse them of the deposits made by pests so that the deposits would not hinder the branches from bearing fruit. In the next verse in John 15:3, the root word *katharos* is used when our Lord went on to say, "You are already clean [*katharos*] because of the word which I have spoken to you."

11. Get into the Word daily and allow it to wash you (see Eph. 5:26). You can read the Word, use a Jesus-centered devotional, or listen to sermons. Just make sure you let the Word wash you! How Jesus cleanses us, whether it's from depression, bitterness, or lying symptoms, is through the washing of the water of His Word that He speaks to us. The more you sit under anointed teaching that lifts you up and washes you, the more fruit you'll bear!

12. The one thing needed is to sit at Jesus' feet and listen to His Word rather than be "distracted with much serving." People who are always worried about many things don't do that *one* thing. Open up your Bible and say, "Lord, speak to me." Do that one thing, and God will take care of all the fires and the many things that you are worried and troubled about will be no more!

CHAPTER 7

2. Because while Israel rests the Rest of Creation, we rest the Rest of Redemption. Our Lord Jesus rose on a Sunday, bringing forth a new order. That's why the early church worshiped on Sunday—the first day of the week (see Acts 20:7).

3. It shows us how God wants our day to begin with rest. Beginning the day in the evening also means the day begins with sleep. This means that when the Jews wake up in the morning, it's not the beginning of the day for them— it's already mid-way through the day, and they start off rested and empowered, having spent time with God and with their family and loved ones.

4. Our Sabbath is a day where we spend time with our Savior, gather as a church to worship Him and hear His Word, and celebrate the intimacy we have with God because our sins have all been taken away at the cross of Jesus. It is a day of rest, and rest is not about doing nothing—it is about making

Him everything, celebrating Him, worshiping Him, and honoring Him with our tithes and offerings.

5. The second priority during Shabbat is relationships with family, loved ones, and friends. At the start of Shabbat, many Jews have an evening meal together with their family and loved ones, purposefully setting aside time each week to gather as a family. I personally find spending time with my family so therapeutic. Shabbat is also a time where parents (usually the fathers) would declare blessings over their children.

6. God did not design man to journey alone. Just as the Jewish people prioritize their family and community, it is important for you to build deep friendships so that when you encounter difficulties in life, your friends can be there to pray for and with you. Likewise, you want to be part of a community where you can step up to believe with your friends for breakthroughs when *they* go through trials.

7. Psalm 92:13 tells us, "Those who are planted in the house of the Lord shall flourish in the courts of our God." Join a local church and find a way to get involved. Don't simply drift into church on Sunday, not make any connections, and leave. Instead, start serving somewhere and start putting your roots down.

8. It was good relationships, not the amount of money one earned or the accolades collected. At the end of the day, happiness is about family, loved ones, and close friends that really matter.

9. It is the importance of sleep and physical rest. As we have seen in Exodus 20:8–11, no work should be done on the Sabbath. God made man last so that man could enjoy everything that He had created. Man was created on the sixth day and God rested on the seventh. Can you see? Man's first full day was God's day of rest. God wanted man to live a life of rest. I would definitely encourage you to observe one day of rest out of seven because your body requires adequate rest.

10. The Sabbath was instituted to point people to Christ. Colossians 2:17 says it is "a shadow of things to come, but the substance is of Christ." The true Sabbath is not a day; it is the lovely person of our Lord Jesus. He is the true substance of the Sabbath!

11. The true substance of the Sabbath rest is not *inactivity*; it is *activity directed by the Spirit of God*, the way our Lord Jesus was led to heal and restore.

He came to give us true rest—rest from our infirmities, rest from the cares that cause us to be bowed down, rest from the bondages of sin!

13. When God tells us to rest, it is for our good. Our bodies are made from the dust of the ground. We must allow our bodies to rest. Otherwise, one way or another, our bodies will find a way to rest, and we might end up in a place where there are many beds to rest on and where people have to come visit us!

14. It means that rest brings God's commanded blessings! When you choose to obey Him and rest, He will command His blessings upon you and on your career. He will command His blessings on your bank account, on your ministry, on your family, on your business, on everything you touch! When you rest and live under God's commanded blessings, you will always have more than enough like the children of Israel.

CHAPTER 8

2. In biblical times, defeated enemies were brought back in chains and the victorious king would sit on his throne and put his feet up on their backs as a sign of victory. When our Lord Jesus rose from the dead and returned to the Father, the Father said, "Sit at My right hand, till I make Your enemies Your footstool." Jesus' throne attitude is to sit, as His Father brings all His defeated enemies under His feet. We, the church, are the body of Christ. This means God Himself is making our enemies our footstool. We can rest in Christ because with each passing day, the defeated enemies of disease, poverty, depression, and all kinds of curses are being put under our feet!

3. Because His work was finished through His one sacrifice on the cross. At the cross, Jesus Christ conquered the enemies of sin, depression, poverty, and premature death. Hebrews tells us that after He sat down, He is "from that time waiting till His enemies are made His footstool." The enemies have *already* been conquered at the cross and since then, God has been putting those enemies under Jesus' feet.

5. Joshua and Caleb had a spirit of rest and they rested in God's promise that He had given them the land. Even in the presence of their enemies and adversities, they were able to stay in rest, because their faith was not established on the giants that they saw, but on God's promises!

6. The Israelites chose to believe that they could not take the land because it was inhabited by giants from the tribe of Anak. In Hebrew, the word *Anak* means "a collar" or "neck chain." A chain around the neck is a yoke that weighs you down. Although they were no longer slaves, they still had a slave mentality. Instead of focusing on God's goodness and promise, they focused on their giant problem—the Anakim—and were weighed down with anxiety and fear. As a result, the whole generation apart from Joshua and Caleb could not enter the land (see Num. 14:29–31) and wandered in the wilderness for forty long years.

7. What the physical land was to the children of Israel in the Old Testament, God's grace and rest are to the believer under the new covenant. Our promised land today is God's rest! God did not deliver the children of Israel out of Egypt to leave them wandering in the wilderness. He brought them out to bring them in! In the same way, God wants to bring you out of lack and into the land of promise and abundance. He wants to bring you out of sickness into robust health. The promised land He wants to bring you into is the place of His rest.

8. God tells us to fear that we fail to enter His rest (see Heb. 4:1). So don't focus on your giants and be stressed out. Place your confidence not in what you see, but in what God has promised in His Word. Rest in the certainty of His Word and He will take care of your giants.

9. God wants you to have the revelation that whatever you need Him to do for you has already been done because Jesus has accomplished all for you. In spite of the giants you see, you can choose to go up and enter the promised land of His rest. When your confidence is in Christ and His finished work, you will be rest-conscious and not giant-conscious!

10. "Sing, O barren, you *who* have not borne! Break forth into singing, and cry aloud, you *who* have not labored with child! For more *are* the children of the desolate than the children of the married woman," says the LORD. "Enlarge the place of your tent, and let them stretch out the curtains of your dwellings; do not spare; lengthen your cords, and strengthen your stakes. For you shall expand to the right and to the left, and your descendants will inherit the nations, and make the desolate cities inhabited."

CHAPTER 9

1. As you reach out to the Lord by faith, allowing Him to work a miracle in your prolonged situation, He is inviting you to step out of your place of fear, worry, and anxiety, and to step into a realm of peace. He is asking you to go *into* peace.

2. "Peace I leave with you, My peace I give to you; not as the world gives do I give to you." The inheritance that Jesus chose to leave with us—the precious gift that He bequeathed to us—was not just any peace, but *His* peace. An inheritance is not put into effect until there is a death and that is why our Lord Jesus laid down His life upon the cross—so that today, His peace is an inheritance we can actively possess.

3. The world tries to achieve "peace" through different means such as meditation, spas, aromatherapy, yoga, and soft music. But this peace can be disrupted by external factors. However, the peace Jesus has given us is not affected by external factors. His peace is a peace that is robust and stable, a peace that surpasses human understanding, a peace that guards our hearts and minds (see Phil. 4:7).

4. He promised to give us a "Helper"—the Holy Spirit. The Greek word for "helper" here is *parakletos,* meaning someone who is "called to one's side" to help. You have a Helper who will teach you all things. This means that instead of being stressed or anxious, you can ask the Holy Spirit to teach you how to handle that situation.

5. You can ask Him to teach you how to handle the situation in your marriage, how to handle your finances, how to meet sales targets, or how to handle your rebellious teenager. He will teach you *all* things. As long as you have received Jesus as your Lord and Savior, you don't have to worry or struggle alone because you have the Holy Spirit who will teach you *all* things.

6. We are told to "listen carefully," to "incline your ear," and to "hear" (see Isa. 55:2–3). As we listen to our Lord through reading the Word, praying and hearing sermons about His finished work, the Bible tells us, "You shall go out with joy, and be led out with peace" (Isa. 55:12). As we listen to His Word on the way to work, while we are doing housework, or as we take a walk in the park, joy and peace will lead us. We will be led out of trouble and worry. We will go out with joy and be led forth by His peace in every area of our lives.

8. The Holy Spirit teaches on the wavelength of peace. Just as you can't listen to a particular radio channel if you are not on the correct wavelength, the Holy Spirit can't teach you if you are not tuned in to His peace. He teaches you all things when you step into the peace that the Prince of Peace has left you with, and the way to step into that peace is to guard your heart from being troubled and afraid.

9. The Greek word for "rule" here is the word *brabeuo*, which means "to arbitrate, decide" or "to act as an umpire." We are to let the peace of God govern our hearts or rule or decide as an umpire. In a tennis match, an umpire decides and has the final say on whether the ball is "in" or "out." There is no point in arguing or protesting a call. In the same way, let us allow the peace of Christ to rule or have the final say in our hearts and in all our decision making.

11. The phrases "go in peace" and "be healed" both carry the Greek present tense, indicating continuous action. So Jesus was actually saying, "You are already healed. Go into peace and remain in peace, and your healing will be permanent."

12. You can trust the Lord for divine healing when you or your loved ones are unwell, but to live in divine health is even better! If a lack of peace had caused the woman's condition, the condition would return if she did not go into and remain in peace. God's best for us is to walk in His divine health and He showed us how to do it—by going into His peace and remaining there!

CHAPTER 10

1. *Shalom* means "welfare," "health, prosperity, peace." It also means "a state of untroubled, undisturbed well-being." This means that what the Lord bequeathed to us as our inheritance was His very own health, His very own provision, and His very own peace.

2. No, it is multiplied in our lives through the *knowledge* of God and of Jesus our Lord, "by the full knowledge of our God, even Jesus, the Lord." The more we know Jesus, the more we will experience His *shalom* being multiplied to us. The Word of God tells us that our Lord Jesus is the Prince of Peace (see Isa. 9:6). As you partake of the beautiful person of Jesus by spending time in His presence and in His Word, His peace will be infused into every fiber of your being. Even when you are confronted with a crisis, His peace will garrison and fortify your heart.

3. Our part is to believe and to walk by faith by not allowing our hearts to be troubled or afraid. Then the peace that is in our spirits will go from our hearts to our souls and into our bodies, and we will experience the fullness of the health, provision, and peace that He paid for us to enjoy!

4. Our heart is the gateway of our spirit. All the *shalom* in our spirit will do us no good if our hearts are clogged with worries, cares, and anxieties. We have to remove those cares. In the Parable of the Sower, our Lord Jesus talked about how the "cares of this world" and the "deceitfulness of riches" are the thorns that choke the Word and cause the hearer to be unfruitful (see Matt. 13:22). Seeds cannot germinate and bear fruit when they are crowded and choked by thorns. In the same way, when our hearts are full of cares, we cannot bear fruit. Our hearts are the valves by which peace flows out—if our hearts are troubled, His peace cannot flow out.

5. By faith in His Word believe that He has already given it to you. Since our Lord Jesus paid the price to bequeath His *shalom* to you, make a decision to possess it by faith and not by what you feel.

6. God's grace gives you all things freely because Jesus has paid for them with His blood. And His peace will retain and keep everything that grace has given.

7. First Peter 5:7 tells you to cast all your cares upon the Lord before verse 8 talks about how the enemy prowls around like a roaring lion, seeking whom he may devour. This tells you that if you are full of care and worry, the enemy can devour you. But if you refuse to allow your heart to be troubled by casting your cares to the Lord, the enemy cannot touch you.

8. Romans 16:20 tells us that "the God of peace will crush Satan under your feet." When you walk in peace and in the power of *Jehovah Shalom*, you can walk all over the enemy and not be afraid!

9. First, cast them to the One who cares for you with deepest affection, the One who laid down His life on the cross for you, and leave those cares and worries in His hands. Second, quote this portion from John 14:27: "Let not your heart be troubled." Your heart will obey the voice of our Lord Jesus as you declare His words.

11. Isaiah 53:5 tells us why: "But He *was* wounded for our transgressions, *He was* bruised for our iniquities; the chastisement for our peace *was* upon Him, and by His stripes we are healed." The chastisement for our *shalom*-peace fell upon Him. In the Hebrew, it says the demand and requirement for the payment of our sins was *exacted* from Christ, so that peace might come on us (see Isa. 53:7 YLT). He bore it all, because He was saying, "I am paying the price for your *shalom*. I am paying the price for your well-being, your wholeness, your completeness, and your health."

12. We did not earn the *shalom* that Jesus bequeathed to us. He paid for it. When He rose from the dead, His first words to the disciples were, "Peace *be* with you," and then He showed them His nail-pierced hands—the receipts of the payment He had made (see John 20:19–20). Because the price has been paid, we have every right to the peace, completeness, welfare, provision, and health that He has bequeathed to us!

CHAPTER 11

1. "Be anxious for nothing, but in everything by prayer and supplication, with thanksgiving, let your requests be made known to God; and the peace of God, which surpasses all understanding, will guard your hearts and minds through Christ Jesus." As you bring your requests to Him and thank Him in faith for the answers, the *peace of God* will guard your heart as well as your mind through Christ Jesus. You may not understand how God's peace works—how it can guard your emotions and reasoning despite the negative circumstances—but that is why it is a true peace that the world cannot give!

2. Peter was so full of peace that he could go to sleep in spite of all that was happening to him and around him. He was in such a deep sleep that he did not even stir when an angel appeared in his cell in a blinding flash of light. In fact, the angel had to strike him on his side to awaken him.

3. Long before our external situations can change, we need the Lord's peace, which surpasses all understanding, to guard our hearts and minds. He has bequeathed this peace to us—a peace that is not as the world gives, but a peace that can prevent our hearts from being troubled or afraid. As we are filled with His peace, what begins on the inside will start affecting our circumstances on the outside!

4. God was saying that my part was to guard my own heart and not guard all the situations around me. And as I guarded my heart and did not allow it to be troubled, He would take care of the situations and every other area of my life. In fact, He would even bring about a miracle if I needed one.

5. The Hebrew word used here for "keep" is *natsar*, which means "to watch, to guard" or "to preserve, to guard from dangers." It is important for us to guard our hearts because out of our hearts spring the issues of life. The NLT Bible says "it determines the course of your life."

7. She kept confessing and declaring, "*It is* well." She kept declaring *shalom*. Even though her emotions were in great turmoil, she did not say what she felt, nor did she say anything about her child's death.

8. The Bible tells us that out of the abundance of the heart, the mouth speaks (see Luke 6:45). One of the ways you can guard your heart is by guarding your mouth and changing the words you speak.

9. When things in your life might not be going as planned, speak forth His *shalom*. When fears and anxieties might be overwhelming you, speak forth His *shalom*. Pray in the Spirit, bring your requests to God, and allow His peace to guard your heart. Keep holding on to His promises and hiding them in the midst of your heart. And as you remain in His *shalom*-peace, get ready for good things to happen. Get ready for your miracle.

10. The frightened disciples assembling behind *doors that were shut* is a picture of how fear happens when your *mouth* is shut. Your mouth is the door to your salvation and the door the devil wants to shut. The Bible tells us that if you confess with your *mouth* that Jesus Christ is Lord, you shall be saved (see Rom. 10:9). You do not have to speak what you see in the natural. Guard your mouth and fill it with unshakable and eternal truths from the Word of God. And the peace of God that surpasses understanding shall guard your heart!

CHAPTER 12

1. We need to understand that we receive all that Jesus purchased for us on the cross *judicially*. He heals us, provides for us, and gives us peace in our hearts and minds *not* because of His mercy, but because these blessings are *legally* and *righteously* ours.

2. Our Lord Jesus, who is altogether perfect and without sin, has finished the work on the cross and answered every accusation that can ever arise, be it from our conscience, the devil, or the claims of divine justice. He took *all* our sins upon His own body. He bore stripe after stripe and punishment after punishment for our sins on *our* behalf. He died in *our* place, conquered death, rose from the dead, and is now seated at the Father's right hand. Today, because of all that He has done, nothing can separate us from the love of God. *Nothing*.

3. Our Lord Jesus was the perfect offering. He has sanctified and cleansed us once for all. Today, we should have no more consciousness of sins because to be full of sin-consciousness would be an insult to the finished work of Christ. Hebrews 10:2 puts it this way: "For the worshipers, once purified, would have had no more consciousness of sins."

5. As believers in Christ, we have been justified—made righteous, acquitted of sin, and declared blameless before God (see Rom. 5:1 AMP). How? By faith. By *believing* that on the cross, Jesus took away all our sins. We are not justified by our works or by our obedience. We are justified by our *believing* and not by our *doing*! Even our best good works cannot make us righteous; only His perfect work can do that.

6. Not at all! In fact, when we receive His righteousness as a gift, we will produce good works in our lives that are the *fruits* of His righteousness. Right believing always produces right living.

7. Stephie saw and declared herself as the righteousness of God in Christ even in the midst of her drug addiction. As she kept putting her trust in God and not in her own willpower, which had failed her time and again, the power of God flowed into her situation and broke the addiction that had bound her for years!

8. Jason started to hope (which according to the Bible is having the *confident expectation of good*) and break free from his fears when he understood more about how good God is and what grace had done for him.

10. This Israelite spent the night in needless anxiety even though nothing was going to happen to his firstborn *because of the blood*. Likewise, many believers today are not enjoying and *possessing* their peace with God even though they *already have* peace with God. The blood is on their doorposts, but they are still fearful because they cannot believe that God is truly that good. Because people hear mixed teachings about God, they can't believe God is really *for* them. They seem to expect the worst to happen in any situation they are in. Let's believe that God is kind toward us and is *for us* and for our good success.

11. The Bible says that Abraham was "strong in faith, giving glory to God" (Rom. 4:20 KJV). The Greek word for "glory" here is *doxa* and one of its meanings is "good opinion." Abraham could be strong in faith because he had a good opinion of God and was fully convinced that what God had promised, He was also able to perform. Let's have greater faith in God's promises to heal, protect, and provide for us.

12. God is love, but He also has inflexible righteousness and unbending holiness. Sin must be punished and the Bible tells us that the wages of sin is death (see Rom. 6:23). That's why our Lord Jesus had to lay down His life on the cross. He did no sin, in Him was no sin, and He knew no sin. But He was punished because He was carrying *our* sins, and only He was qualified to do this. At the cross, God's love blended with God's justice. Righteousness and mercy met. Mercy and truth kissed. At the cross, the divine exchange took place—Jesus was punished so that we could go free, be blessed, and be accepted!

13. Thorns represent the curse. Our Lord Jesus took our curse of depression. He took our curse of stress and anxiety. He took our filthy imaginations. He took our dark and evil thoughts. He took it all and He paid it all so that He could crown us with His peace that surpasses understanding. This means you don't have to live under that cloud of despair anymore or allow those thoughts of hatred toward yourself to define you. You don't have to live in perpetual shame and condemnation.

14. When we keep our minds *stayed* and fixed on our Lord Jesus, the Word of God tells us that He will keep us in perfect peace. Today, let's keep our minds fixed on His sacrifice, stayed on the price that He paid, and focused on His finished work. We can never do enough to merit any of His blessings. But praise be to God, He has done it all—we can rest. We can let go. We can depend wholly on our Savior!

CHAPTER 13

1. The pillar of cloud that had led them in the wilderness moved behind them and stood between them and the Egyptian army. As such the enemies of Israel could not come near them at all that night. But God did not just hold back Israel's enemies. The foreboding sea that had blocked their path was rent in two as God opened up the Red Sea for His people.

2. No matter how difficult the situation, it is not over. God can *still* turn things around for you, just like He did for the children of Israel.

3. The Lord can prepare a table before you *in the presence* of your enemies (see Ps. 23:5). The Red Sea did not disappear, just as your problems will not simply vanish. But even if you are faced with a sea of problems, the Lord can split it apart for you. Your part is to stand still and see the salvation of the Lord!

4. The Bible is saying *stand still and see Jesus!* Fix your eyes on Him and not on your challenges. Let your mind be stayed on His goodness and faithfulness. Get hold of sermons that unveil Jesus. Listen to them day and night, for just by beholding Jesus, the waters will part before you. Just by beholding Jesus, you will come out of your Egypt.

5. When you stand still *in Him*, you are actively putting your faith in His love for you and allowing the Lord Himself to fight your battles. Standing still is about letting go and allowing His abundant supply to flow. Our worrying cannot add even one cubit to our stature, but our *trusting* in Him can result in miracles. In the midst of your trial, stand still *inwardly* and look to the Lord to fight for you.

6. He will provide practically for your needs. If you are trusting Him for better clientele or more business leads, He can supernaturally cause doors of opportunity to open for you. If a particular revenue stream has dried up, or perhaps you need creativity and ideas to flow for that upcoming project or business campaign, the Lord can cause what you need to gush forth from unexpected sources. Put your trust in Him and He will provide exceedingly, abundantly, above all that you ask or think (see Eph. 3:20)!

7. While it is important that we do our best and be excellent in all that we set our hands to, our trust and dependence have to be on the Lord and not on our hard work and efforts. Our blessings are not dependent on the economy, on the state of the property market, or on the stock market. God can bless us in the midst of our wilderness and He can bless us in the presence of our enemies. But if our dependence is on ourselves and not on Him, we can hit or squeeze rocks all we want and the only thing that will flow out is our own blood!

8. Stop worrying. He feeds even the birds of the air and He clothes the lilies of the field. He will take care of you. You can have rest in your mind and stop allowing anxiety to dictate how you live your life. Stop holding on to all your cares so tightly and let them go into the loving hands of your Savior!

9. "I'm not going to worry about this! My Lord Jesus is going to handle it."

10. Because what the first Adam brought about in the first garden had to be finished off in another garden by the last Adam. When Adam fell, God said to him, "By the sweat of your brow you will eat your food" (Gen. 3:19 NIV). So Jesus sweating great drops of blood from His brow means that we are redeemed from stress, anxiety, and from every oppressive thought and crippling lie that torments our minds!

11. He redeemed all of us from the curse of sweat in our thinking, from laboring and struggling that is full of stress and trouble but with no results. We can work but be relaxed! You can labor without stress and enjoy your Savior.

12. The Lord says to you, "Do not remember the former things, nor consider the things of old. Behold, I will do a new thing, now it shall spring forth; shall you not know it? I will even make a road in the wilderness *and* rivers in the desert" (Isa. 43:18–19). He will give you the grace to forget the former things because He is getting ready to do a *new* thing in your life.

13. Stand still and keep your eyes on the Lord Jesus. Don't wait till you see the manifestation of your promise to rejoice. "Sing, O barren!" the Bible declares (Isa. 54:1). Rest and rejoice in His finished work, even when you still see that negative report. Break forth into singing and praising God even when you have not seen your desired results yet! Then get ready for your miracle. God is about to make roadways in the wilderness and bring forth rivers in the desert for you. He will make a way where there seems to be no way!

CHAPTER 14

1. It was rest. God did not choose David to build Him a temple because David was *a man of war*. Instead, He wanted someone who was *a man of rest*, someone whose life was marked by peace and quietness. And so He chose David's son, Solomon, whose name in Hebrew, *Shelomoh*, means "peace."

2. The number one quality to successfully building God's house is *rest*. People of war—people who are always fighting and striving—will struggle to build anything. Whether you are involved in building a business, negotiating contracts, entering a new partnership, or raising a family, remember this, God has called you to be a person of rest.

3. God does not want you to waste your time wringing your hands being worried, eating the bread of adversity and sorrows. Don't stay up past midnight every day, or keep pushing yourself to work long hours without any rest. Stop being anxious and stressed out about your family, your job, or the tasks that you have ahead of you. Stay in His rest and win the battle over insomnia. The Bible tells us that He gives His beloved sleep. And not only does He give you sleep, He gives to you what you need *while* you are sleeping—He gave Solomon wisdom as he slept.

4. You are God's beloved and He wants to give you sleep and give to you as you sleep. Don't stay up and stay stressed out—let Him who neither slumbers nor sleeps take over (see Ps. 121:4). Go to sleep when it is time for bed because that is faith in action. You can rest because *the Lord* is building the house and the Lord is guarding the city. The Lord is building your business, your ministry, your career, your family, and your health!

5. Because God is the only One who can build and guard every area of *your* life. If the Lord isn't building, we would be laboring in vain anyway. But know He loves you, is working behind the scenes for you, and wants you to enjoy sweet and uninterrupted sleep as you rest in His love for you.

6. You don't have to be worried about losing out. Instead of choking the Lord's supply by holding on with our own strength, you can let go and have a good opinion of God. Trust that He is the God who goes before you and is your rear guard. If something does not work out—a relationship, a job opportunity, the purchase of a house you had been eyeing—then believe that the Lord is setting you up for something greater!

8. Because Naomi knew that Boaz had fallen in love with Ruth and he *would not rest* until he had concluded the matter of her redemption. And the result was that Boaz married Ruth and they became the great-grandparents of King David and became a part of the natural ancestry of our Lord Jesus.

9. Whatever you are going through today, you can put your trust in your Redeemer. You can sit still because He will not rest until He has redeemed you from that trouble. God told the children of Israel, "I will redeem you with an outstretched arm" (Ex. 6:6), and that is literally how our Lord Jesus redeemed us, with His arms stretched out on the cross to redeem us from the slave market of sin, poverty, and curses.

10. Naomi said to Ruth, "Shall I not seek rest for thee, that it may be well with thee?" (Ruth 3:1 KJV). As we stay in His rest, the Lord will cause all things to go well with us!

11. The Lord sees your desire to build Him a house. But He wants to build *your* house. The Lord delights in blessing you. He will command His blessings upon you in your ministry, in your health, in your marriage, in your parenting, and in your relationships. He delights in raining down His grace and showing you His goodness. Why? Because He loves you.

12. The more troubles you put in His hands, the more you rest in Him and the more He works. Focus only on one labor—entering the rest! Come to a place of quietness and of knowing that when you sit still, the Man will not rest until He has concluded the matter! We can only flow in God's supply of whatever we need when we rest in Him.

13. He finished His work of qualifying us, bearing the punishment of all our sins, delivering us from the power of darkness, and redeeming us from the curse of the law. It is all finished. He has done it all for us. He finally found His rest in saving you, in finishing the work for you. He found His rest in qualifying you by His blood for every blessing of God. Today, you can rest. You don't have to earn healing, or blessings, or rest—you only have to receive it!

CHAPTER 15

1. They failed to enter because the word they heard was "not mixed with faith." Everything that we receive from God is by faith. We were saved by grace through faith (see Eph. 2:8). We are healed by faith in the name of Jesus (see Acts 3:16). Our Lord Jesus Himself told many of those whom He had healed, "your faith has made you well" (see Mark 5:34, 10:52; Luke 17:19). In fact, the Bible tells us that without faith, it is impossible to please God (see Heb. 11:6).

2. "Faith *comes* by hearing, and hearing by the word of God" (Rom. 10:17). If you study the word "God" here, you will see that it is translated from the Greek word *Christos*, meaning Christ. In other words, faith comes by hearing the word of *Christ*. Faith comes when we talk about the person and work of our Lord Jesus. Faith comes when, despite knowing that we have failed, we hear that we can still receive the abundance of grace and gift of righteousness through Christ (see Rom. 5:17), and begin living the victorious life. Jesus is the author and finisher of our faith (see Heb. 12:2). Don't try to get faith by focusing on faith. Faith comes by *hearing and hearing*—hearing and hearing and hearing and hearing the word of Christ!

3. The Bible makes it clear that faith comes by hearing a *preacher* who brings the word of Christ. The delivery system that God chose for us to receive His blessings and miracles is by "the foolishness of preaching." A preacher simply preaches the gospel of grace and people are saved. Faith is imparted as the people listen. A preacher preaches the power of the cross and people are healed from their afflictions. They are set free from anxiety attacks and rescued from addictions that have bound them—as the Word goes forth!

4. Luke 5:15 tells us that "great multitudes came together to hear, and to be healed by Him." The blueprint of God is to hear and then be healed. We hear teaching and preaching, and we are healed. The Bible tells us, "And Jesus went about all Galilee, teaching in their synagogues, preaching the gospel of the kingdom, and healing all kinds of sickness and all kinds of disease among the people" (Matt. 4:23). Beloved, it doesn't matter what your affliction is or what challenge torments you. They all have to bow before the name of Jesus because He is "far above all principality and power and might and dominion, and every name that is named" (Eph. 1:21).

5. In the original Hebrew, it is actually a *shama* or hearing heart—a heart that listens. And this pleased the Lord so much that He not only gave Solomon what he had asked for, but He also gave him what he had not asked for: "both riches and honor" (1 Kings 3:13).

6. Mary "seated herself at the Lord's feet and was *continually* listening to His teaching" (Luke 10:39 AMP). She was *hearing and hearing* the Lord's teaching! When we do the "one thing" that Mary did, we will not be worried and troubled about *many things*.

7. You might not have been hearing and hearing (present continuous tense) the word of Christ. Don't make the mistake of thinking that because you have heard a few sermons about God's grace you know all about it. It is not enough to have *heard*. Just as you have to keep eating food to live, food for your faith comes by hearing and hearing.

8. Satan comes immediately to take away the Word that was sown. He does not want God's Word to stay in our hearts for even one day because he knows how powerful the seeds of God's Word are once they take root. As long as the Word does not take root, we still stumble when tribulation arises.

9. This fight is not against Satan directly but is the fight to believe that God has given to us. We fight to walk by faith and not by sight! When we are in faith, the devil is defeated. Every temptation to snare us back into stress and worry is an attempt to knock us from our place of faith in Christ.

10. Fear causes us to focus on all the problems we can see—in the news, in our lives, at our place of work. Faith helps us to focus on what God sees— beyond the bad news, the physical symptoms, and any giants in front of us. The Word of God tells us that "the things which are seen *are* temporary, but the things which are not seen *are* eternal" (2 Cor. 4:18). By faith we see that all those problems are only temporal!

11. It is not enough to have heard a biblical promise that addresses a fear or problem. We need to keep hearing and hearing until His promises take root in our hearts. And when that happens, we shall "produce a harvest of thirty, sixty, or even a hundred times as much as had been planted" (Mark 4:20 NLT)!

12. As you take time to listen to and wait on the Lord, may He renew your strength and cause you to run and not be weary, to walk and not faint!

13. The word "heard" is in the imperfect tense in the original Greek text, meaning the man was a "habitual hearer of Paul's preaching" and "heard *repeatedly* the teaching of the Gospel." He kept on hearing and hearing until one day when Paul discerned that "he had faith to be healed," and he received his miracle at Paul's command to stand up.

14. According to Acts 14:3, Paul and Barnabas were preaching "the word of His grace" and God was bearing witness to what they preached, granting signs and wonders to be done by their hands!

CHAPTER 16

1. *Many* rivers, not one. What a beautiful picture of constant provision, with *rivers* of water sustaining and refreshing you all the time. Even if one river runs dry, there are other rivers flowing. And you did not just randomly *grow* by the river. Someone *planted* you! Surely the One who planted you will also tend to and take care of you!

2. It means not being barren in any way, but fruitful in every area, including in your finances, in your body, and in your ministry. Your leaves shall not wither; instead, they shall be perennially green, fresh, and full of sap. What this speaks of is that you will always be young, strong, and full of life and energy. Leaves in the Bible also speak of healing, meaning your health will be evergreen; it will not fail you!

3. It goes on to say "whatever he does shall prosper." What a powerful promise! Whatever you do shall prosper! Even if you make a mistake, the Lord can cause it to prosper!

4. He savors and enjoys the Word of the Lord. Spending time in the Word is not something he does legalistically, but because he does it with revelation, it gives him delight, or "great pleasure" and "a high degree of gratification," such that he meditates on God's Word day and night!

5. The Hebrew word for *meditate* is *hagah*, which means to utter or mutter, to speak in a low voice as is often done by those who are musing. God's way of meditation is not just to think in your head, but to also mutter with your mouth. As you meditate on and mutter God's Word to yourself, you are hearing and hearing the word of Christ!

6. God tells Joshua that the Book of the Law shall not depart from his *mouth*—it's your *mouth*, not so much your mind, which you use in meditation. Take a word of Scripture and mutter it under your breath day and night "that you may observe to do according to all that is written in it," and you will prosper and have good success.

7. Prosperity does not refer to finances only. It touches every area of your life, including your relationships, your family, your peace of mind, and your health. And to have *good* success implies that there is *bad* success. If you are financially "successful" but have no time to enjoy being with your family and your friends, and are always working and don't get to do the things you enjoy, that's not good success.

8. After we read God's Word, we can bring it up and chew on it again and again. During the day, there are always pockets of idle time when we can bring up verses and promises that can feed us all over again, ruminating on the Word until we have obtained all the nutrients and extracted all the water from it. God wants us to ruminate on His inexhaustible Word throughout the day and continuously feed on His truths until we have extracted all the nourishment we can from even a single verse.

9. It can be as simple as an index card with Bible verses that you carry with you and pull out to read and chew on for nourishment during the day. Or use a Bible app in your smartphone. If you have worrisome thoughts, take a verse and quote it, and chew on it over and over.

11. As you meditate upon teaching and doctrine and give yourselves wholly to them, it says that you will see "profiting" in your life. What you have on the inside will be manifested on the outside so that it becomes obvious to everybody—your profiting in all areas is demonstrated to all.

CHAPTER 17

1. Make it a game to catch each other being anxious and remind each other not to let your hearts be troubled. Decide that both of you will always be quick to forgive each other and to let go of any hurts to the Lord. Find Christ-centered messages that you can listen to together and share the portions that spoke to you with your spouse. If you are going through a health or financial challenge, find promises in God's Word that you can meditate on as a couple. Ask the Lord, who is always for you, to help you both keep Him in your conversations and to always keep Him in the center of your marriage.

2. Our Lord Jesus said, "If two of you agree on earth concerning anything that they ask, it will be done for them by My Father in heaven" (Matt. 18:19). Together, you can agree to cast all your cares to the Lord about providing for your family, about your children's education, and about the bills to be paid. Together, you can agree to stay in rest instead of being stressed up and flustered. Remind each other that the Lord Himself fights your battles against any chronic sickness, any lack of time for each other, and against any addiction that has put a strain on your marriage. As you keep focusing on the Lord Jesus and His finished work instead of each other, He will draw you closer to your spouse and cause your marriage to be stronger than ever!

3. In Hebrew, "hearken diligently" is made up of *shama shama,* which literally means "listen, listen." We have seen how important listening is because the blessings of God come by us listening. When we *shama shama,* we can, in growing measure experience the Lord's promise of "days of heaven upon the earth," which is in the context of family life.

4. God ordained marriage to be a powerful covenant. The Bible declares that one can chase a thousand, but two can put ten thousand to flight (see Deut. 32:30). There is exponential power in a marriage.

6. Demands, stress, and burdens can have a negative impact on our relationships and marriages. Worry and anxiety can put a large strain on our marriages and even affect intimacy. Babies come. There are diapers to change and mouths to feed, and the wine runs out. There are bosses to please, deadlines to meet, and the wine runs out.

7. His name is Jesus. The Bible tells us that "a threefold cord is not quickly broken" (Eccl. 4:12). When you invite Him to take center place in your marriage and you each draw from Him instead of constantly making withdrawals from each other, your marriage can be strengthened instead of becoming depleted—even when demands pile up.

8. Only the Lord can take that place. Your spouse cannot be God. When you keep your eyes on the Lord instead of each other, you can minister to each other out of His unlimited strength and grace, instead of drawing from each other. When you invite Him to take center place in your marriage, He can cause that which is tasteless and bland to become sweet and intoxicating. He can infuse your marriage with more passion and love than when your marriage first started. He will ensure that the wine never runs out and that you are supplied exceedingly, abundantly, above all that you ask or think (see Eph. 3:20)!

9. As you invite Him into your marriage, He declares to you today, "I will restore to you the years that the swarming locust has eaten" (Joel 2:25)!

10. God reminded David that He had supplied him abundantly in other areas. But David had not asked God to supply what he needed in the area of his marriage. Many people have the mistaken idea that God is concerned with more "important" things like salvation, and they fail to bring more "mundane" areas like grace for their marriage to the Lord. God cares for your marriage and He wants to supply His grace for your marriage. When you try to provide for yourself, you will end up in a deeper problem.

11. We should always be asking the Lord for more of His grace in our marriages. If you are not satisfied with your marriage—the passion has run out and there is no more joy in your relationship—ask the Lord for more of His grace in your marriage. But let's be clear that He won't give you a relationship outside of your marriage. He will give you and your spouse a fresh desire for each other and infuse that which has become bland with His sweet love!

12. Even if you have failed, the Lord can still turn things around because of His grace. As you experience His undeserved and unmerited love, the Lord can cause you to be an even better spouse than before. You don't deserve it, but at the cross, He paid the price for you to experience His blessings in your marriage. He was your trespass offering, bearing every punishment that you deserved so that you can walk in every blessing that He deserved (see Eph. 2:4–7).

13. Your part is to let go of all your trying, all your worrying, and all your regrets. Let go and rest in His finished work. As you put your trust in Him instead of all your efforts, His miracle working power will begin to flow and you will see Him do a new thing in your marriage.

14. As they kept on hearing about what Jesus had done for them, the water turned to wine. Love returned to their marriage and their relationship became better than it was before!

CHAPTER 18

1. God first wants *us* to lay up His words in *our* hearts and souls—to meditate and to chew on His words over and over again until they sink into our hearts and souls.

2. In our daily lives—by talking about His words whether we are sitting down in our own house or walking along outside, when we are getting up and when we lie down. As we spend time personally meditating on His Word and "muttering" them in the presence of our children, that's how they will learn! And because of our examples, they will come to know of the goodness of God! This applies especially for younger children.

3. We are to teach them about Jesus. The Hebrew word that is left untranslated is actually two alphabets, *Aleph* and *Tav*, which is the signature of our Lord Jesus. *Aleph* is the first letter of the Hebrew alphabet, while *Tav* is the last letter. In the book of Revelation, Jesus told John "I am the Alpha and the Omega, *the* Beginning and *the* End" (Rev. 1:8). Alpha is the first letter of the Greek alphabet while omega is the last. But Jesus would have spoken in Hebrew to His fellow Jews: "I am *Aleph* and I am *Tav*." God wants us to teach our children *Jesus*!

5. You are sandwiching your children in the Lord's anointing, like what the Shunammite woman did when she put her dead son on Elisha's bed, which was soaked with the anointing. Later, Elisha stretched himself out on top of the child, putting the boy in a divine anointed sandwich—anointing below and anointing upon—and the boy was brought back to life. This is a picture of how covering our children with the anointing and surrounding them with the Word of God can cause them to become spiritually alive.

6. You may not see fruits immediately but in due season, your children will bear fruit! By faith, keep on telling them about your wonderful Jesus, who loves them unconditionally even when they fail. Keep on bringing them to church, even if they don't understand the teachings. Our Lord Jesus said, "For where two or three are gathered together in My name, I am there in the midst of them" (Matt. 18:20). He is in the midst of your children—and His presence will guide and guard them.

7. The best thing we can do is to let go of them and prayerfully release them into the Lord's arms of love. Stop trying by your own efforts to change your children. As you focus on laying up God's Word in your heart and teaching your children all about Jesus, believe that the blessing of experiencing days of heaven upon the earth will come upon your children. Apply the cross to whatever challenges your children are faced with—every sickness, every rejection, and every struggle was put on the body of Jesus on the cross. Keep on meditating on His finished work and pointing them to Him. Let go and put your trust in the Lord.

8. Too often we put our faith in the decrees that doctors, teachers, or psychologists have made about our children. Let's remember to put our faith not in these experts and their words that can fail, but in the One whose words will not return to Him void (see Isa. 55:11).

9. It is a place of salvation, safety, and deliverance. When you let go of your cares about your children, you are not releasing them into treacherous waters. You are letting your children go and placing them into the Ark. Those who were in Noah's ark were saved from the waters of judgment, so the ark is a picture of our Lord Jesus! You are letting go of your cares about your children and putting your children into the hands of Jesus, who will *never* fail.

10. He can cause them to be at the right place at the right time and save them from destruction. He can bring the right people into their lives who will take care of them, teach them, and provide for them as if they were their own children! Jochebed was even paid to take care of her own son, and Moses was sponsored by the treasury of Pharaoh, the same man who had ordered his death.

11. The Bible says that our children will be taught by the Lord and that not only shall they have peace, their peace shall be great! The Hebrew word for "peace" here is *shalom*, which also means completeness, soundness, welfare, and peace. You can stand on this promise that your children can be completely healthy, whole, and well. Lay hold of this truth that they can walk in supernatural peace—even if the circumstances around them may not look good.

CHAPTER 19

1. The Hebrew word for "sound," describing the heart in this verse, is the word *marpe* meaning "a healing" or "cure." This tells you that when your heart is at peace, when it is tranquil and peaceful, it becomes a healing heart that gives life to your body! In other words, if you want to live long, have a relaxed attitude. Let your heart not be troubled, neither let it be afraid (see John 14:27)!

2. *Rapha* means "to heal," and this is the same word the Lord uses to refer to Himself as our *Jehovah Rapha*, "the LORD who heals you" (Ex. 15:26). If we take it one step deeper, we see that *rapha* is closely related to the root verb *raphah*, which means "to relax, to let go." In other words, in Hebrew, *healing* is closely tied to the act of *relaxing*. Doesn't this remind you of letting go of your worries, relaxing your grip, and allowing His supply to flow through those pipes from heaven? Doesn't this also remind you of the unforced, effortless rhythm of grace?

3. Healing comes when the head and mouth speak of the sacrifice! The more we meditate on and speak about the sacrifice that our Lord Jesus made on the cross, the more we will walk in the health that He paid for us to possess. If you are trusting the Lord for healing today, keep on thinking and speaking of His sacrifice. Keep on meditating on verses that speak of His finished work.

4. "My son, give attention to my words; incline your ear to my sayings. Do not let them depart from your eyes; keep them in the midst of your heart; for they *are* life to those who find them, and health to all their flesh."

5. He tells us to give attention to His words and to incline our ears to His sayings. He exhorts us to not let His words depart from our eyes, to keep our focus and attention on *His* words. Whatever negative reports or diagnosis we may have received, let's keep our eyes on His words and never lose sight of them. Let's allow His promises to penetrate deep into our hearts. When we do that, His words "*are* life to those who find them, and health to all their flesh."

By the way, the Hebrew word for health here is *marpe*. God's Word is healing to *all* our flesh. It is healing to our eyes, kidneys, bones, skin, and lungs. It is healing to *all* our flesh! Not a single part of our bodies will be left untouched by the healing power of God's Word!

6. It says, "Do not look at the things which are seen, but at the things which are not seen. For the things which are seen *are* temporary, but the things which are not seen *are* eternal." That medical report is temporal and natural; God's Word is eternal and supernatural. Man is subject to failures and mistakes; God never fails. The more you think and speak forth His Word, the more you will experience His supernatural healing!

7. As you hold on to His Word, keep believing for your complete healing too in the mighty name of Jesus. Be still. Cease striving and know that He is God. Stand still and see the salvation, the help, and the deliverance of your God. He has not forgotten you. At the name of Jesus, whatever condition you might have bows to Him. So in the name of Jesus, be healed. Right now, that same Holy Spirit that raised Jesus Christ from the dead quickens your body. Receive that infusion of strength. Receive renewal of youth like the eagle's and restoration of strength in Jesus' name!

8. Christ has redeemed us from every curse (see Gal. 3:13), and He wants us to enjoy days of heaven on earth in every area of our lives (see Deut. 11:21). This means that even as we advance in age, it is not God's will for us to live with sickness and pain.

9. At the age of eighty-five, Caleb declared, "I *am as* strong this day as on the day that Moses sent me; just as my strength *was* then, so now *is* my strength for war" (Josh. 14:11). Moses was 120 years old when he died, and "yet his eyesight was clear, and he was as strong as ever" (Deut. 34:7 NLT). When Sarah was in her sixties, the Egyptians saw "that she *was* very beautiful" (Gen. 12:14) and took her for Pharaoh's harem. When she was in her nineties, Abimelech, king of Gerar, also took her for his harem (see Gen. 20:2). Now, these were heathen kings who had their pick of the most beautiful women in their land. What does that tell you? God renewed her youth.

10. He attributed it to three causes, one of which was His love for the Scriptures and the constant recuperative power they exercised upon his whole being. There's a reviving, purifying, resuscitating, rejuvenating, and prospering power in God's Word!

11. Müller said, "For more than seventy years I have not been anxious," even though he was responsible for providing for and taking care of over *ten thousand* orphans during his lifetime. He said, "It is the great privilege of the child of God not to be anxious. And it is possible to attain to it even in this life; yea, in the midst of great difficulties, great trials." Müller was able to not be anxious because he said, "I have rolled my burdens on the Lord, and He has carried them for me. The result of that has been that 'the peace of God, which passeth all understanding,' has kept my heart and mind."

12. It says that the Lord "*is* your life and the length of your days." The length of your days is a person—Jesus! Our longevity and the blessings we can enjoy are not based on what we need to do but dependent on Him who is all-powerful, all-knowing, and best of all, all-loving! Because of Him, we can

have a security that is unshakable, a joy unspeakable, and peace that surpa.
understanding!

13. The Hebrew word for "salvation" is *yeshua*, the name of Jesus in Hebrew. In other words, the verse can be read as, "With long life I will satisfy him, and show him My *Yeshua*," or "My Jesus." The more of Jesus you see in the Word, the more you will live long. And God gives you long life so that you see more and more and more of His Son.

CHAPTER 20

1. Even if everything around you seems to have been shaken, there is an unshakable Rock that is higher than you. His name is Jesus. His everlasting love toward you will *never* fail. He is the strong tower you can run to when your enemies surround you. In the shelter of His wings, you can safely rest.

3. The Bible tells us that "when he saw *that*, he arose and ran for his life" (1 Kings 19:3). Elijah—the man of faith—started to walk by sight. He got snared by the visible things that are temporal and lost sight of the invisible God, who is eternal.

4. Elijah forgot the God who led him to Cherith. He forgot who brought the ravens that fed him by day and by evening. He forgot about the widow whom God commanded to feed him. And he forgot about the barrel of meal that never ran out and the jar of oil that never ran dry. He forgot the God of the resurrection who raised the boy from the dead through him. He forgot the God who answered by fire and the rain that followed.

5. Elijah also became depressed and suicidal, praying that he might die.

6. In most instances in the Old Testament, "the angel of the LORD" refers to the pre-incarnate appearance of Christ. Just as the resurrected Jesus cooked breakfast for His hungry disciples (see John 21:9), the Lord Jesus appeared to Elijah and provided for him, saying, "Arise *and* eat, because the journey *is* too great for you" (1 Kings 19:7). My friend, He loves you, He understands how you feel, and He cares for you intimately and practically. Never doubt that.

7. He feeds us with His Word. Keep partaking of Jesus in the Word. Keep eating of the bread of life. See the Lord Jesus breaking bread for you and saying to you, "Take, eat; this is My body" (Matt. 26:26). One word from God can cause you to go in His strength.

9. He seeks us out to strengthen us during our time of discouragement. It may be through His Word, a note from a friend, or the pages of this study guide. His message is, "Be strong and of good courage, do not fear nor be afraid of them; for the Lord your God, He *is* the One who goes with you. He will not leave you nor forsake you" (Deut. 31:6). He is on the journey with you!

10. When you can't see, trust. Trust in the invisible, infallible God who loves you! Jesus said, "I am with you always, *even* to the end of the age" (Matt. 28:20). The Lord Jesus Himself is with you. Always. Right now.

11. The Lord was not in the earthquake, the wind, or the fire. He was in the still, small voice. If you study this verse in Hebrew, this refers to a calm whisper of gentleness. What's that? It's the ministry of grace. Don't look for God in outward manifestations. He is in the gentle whisper that speaks right to your heart.

EXTRA RESOURCES

To hear Joseph Prince preach on the biblical principles and truths shared in each chapter of this book, please check out the following audio messages at JosephPrince.com/LetGo:

Chapter 1: Let Go
It's Time to Let Go!
Your Only Battle Today Is the Fight to Remain at Rest

Chapter 2: Just Look at the Birds
Let Go and Let God Flow
God's Rest for the Rest of Your Life
Never Alone, Always Cared For

Chapter 3: Experience His Quality Life and Health
Becoming Stress-Free and Healthy
Never Alone, Always Cared For

Chapter 4: The Way to Living Worry-Free
Becoming Stress-Free and Healthy
Live the Let-Go Life!

Chapter 5: The Rhythm of Rest
Living by the Unforced Rhythms of Grace
Rest Is the Promised Land of the Believer
Live Stress-Free by His Spirit

Chapter 6: Walking in the Rhythm of Grace
Let Go and Flow in the Vine Life

Chapter 7: Rest Brings God's Commanded Blessings
Jesus Our True Jubilee and Sabbath
Restful Increase versus Stressful Increase

Chapter 8: Have a Throne Attitude
Have a Throne Attitude—Rest Until God Makes Your Enemies Your Footstool
Your Only Battle Today Is the Fight to Remain at Rest

Chapter 9: Tune In to Peace
Peace Keeps What Grace Gives
Live Stress-Free by His Spirit
If It's a Miracle You Need, a Miracle You'll Get—If You Remain in Peace

Chapter 10: All-Encompassing *Shalom*
If It's a Miracle You Need, a Miracle You'll Get—If You Remain in Peace
Live the Let-Go Life!
Peace Keeps What Grace Gives

Chapter 11: Above All Things, Guard Your Heart
Rest Is the Promised Land of the Believer
If It's a Miracle You Need, a Miracle You'll Get—If You Remain in Peace
Hidden Secrets to Health in the Hebrew Language

Chapter 12: Peace in Your Conscience
Jesus Became Your Overpayment to Give You Settled Peace
Hidden Secrets to Health in the Hebrew Language
Receive Your 120 Percent Restoration Today!

Chapter 13: Stand Still
Why the Finished Work Begins in Your Mind

Chapter 14: Becoming a Person of Rest
When You Sit Still He Will Not Rest

Chapter 15: Hear Your Way to Victory

The One Thing that Brings Success in Every Area

The Secret of Hearing that Brings Untold Blessings

Chapter 16: The One Thing that Brings Success in Every Area

Meditating on God's Word—The Key to True Prosperity

Chapter 17: Experiencing Blessings in Marriage

Christ Is the Centre of Happy Marriages #1

Receive God's Grace for All of Life's Demands

Chapter 18: Stress-Free Parenting

The One Thing that Brings Success in Every Area

Blessings upon the Whole Household #2

Chapter 19: Let Go and Live Long

Hidden Secrets to Health in the Hebrew Language

The Health-Giving Power of a Relaxed Heart

Chapter 20: You Are Not Alone

Win Over Discouragement, Depression, and Burnout

WE WOULD LIKE TO HEAR FROM YOU

If you have a testimony to share after reading this book, please send it to us via JosephPrince.com/testimony.

STAY CONNECTED WITH JOSEPH

Connect with Joseph through these social media channels and receive daily inspirational teachings:

Facebook.com/JosephPrince
Twitter.com/JosephPrince
Youtube.com/JosephPrinceOnline
Instagram: @JosephPrince

FREE DAILY E-MAIL DEVOTIONAL

Sign up for Joseph's FREE daily e-mail devotional at JosephPrince.com/meditate and receive bite-size inspirations to help you grow in grace.

BOOKS BY JOSEPH PRINCE

Live the Let-Go Life

One of the most essential books Joseph has written, *Live the Let-Go Life* is the go-to resource for anyone who wants to find freedom from the stress and anxieties of modern living. Instead of letting worries, stress, and all their negative effects rule your life, discover how you can cast all your cares to the One who cares about you like no other, and experience His practical supply for every need. You'll find simple yet powerful truths and tools to help you put worry and anxiety under your feet and experience greater health and well-being. Learn how you can tune in to God's peace, walk daily in His unforced rhythm of grace, and find yourself living healthier, happier, and having time for the important things in life!

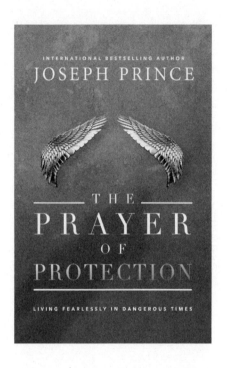

The Prayer of Protection

We live in dangerous times. A time in which terrorist activities, pandemics, and natural calamities are on the rise. But there is good news. God has given us a powerful prayer of protection—Psalm 91—through which we and our families can find safety and deliverance from every snare of the enemy. In *The Prayer of Protection*, discover a God of love and His impenetrable shield of protection that covers everything that concerns you, and start living fearlessly in these dangerous times!

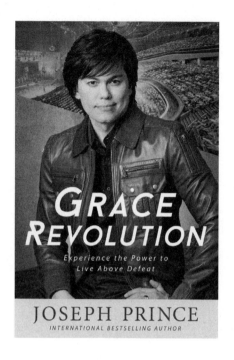

Grace Revolution

Experience the revolution that is sweeping across the world! In *Grace Revolution*, Joseph Prince offers five powerful keys that will help you experience firsthand the grace revolution in your own life, and live above defeat. See how these keys can work easily for you, as you read inspiring stories of people who experienced amazing and lasting transformations when they encountered the real Jesus and heard the unadulterated gospel. Whatever your challenge today, begin to step away from defeat and take a massive leap toward your victory. Get your copy today and let the revolution begin in your life!

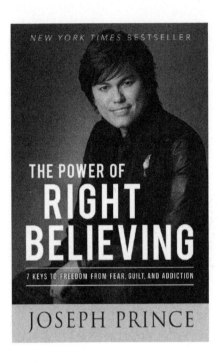

The Power of Right Believing

Experience transformation, breakthroughs, and freedom today through the power of right believing! This book offers seven practical and powerful keys that will help you find freedom from all fears, guilt, and addictions. See these keys come alive in the many precious testimonies you will read from people around the world who have experienced breakthroughs and liberty from all kinds of bondages. Win the battle for your mind through understanding the powerful truths of God's Word and begin a journey of victorious living and unshakable confidence in God's love for you!

Destined to Reign

This pivotal and quintessential book on the grace of God will change your life forever! Join Joseph Prince as he unlocks foundational truths to understanding God's grace and how it alone sets you free to experience victory over every adversity, lack, and destructive habit that is limiting you today. Be uplifted and refreshed as you discover how reigning in life is all about Jesus and what He has already done for you. Start experiencing the success, wholeness, and victory that you were destined to enjoy!

Unmerited Favor

This follow-up book to *Destined to Reign* is a must-read if you want to live out the dreams that God has birthed in your heart! Building on the foundational truths of God's grace laid out in *Destined to Reign*, *Unmerited Favor* takes you into a deeper understanding of the gift of righteousness that you have through the cross and how it gives you a supernatural ability to succeed in life. Packed with empowering new covenant truths, *Unmerited Favor* will set you free to soar above your challenges and lead an overcoming life as God's beloved today.

ABOUT THE AUTHOR

JOSEPH PRINCE is a leading voice in proclaiming the gospel of grace to a whole new generation of believers and leaders. He is the senior pastor of New Creation Church in Singapore, a vibrant and dynamic church with a congregation of more than 30,000 attendees. He separately heads Joseph Prince Ministries, one of the fastest-growing television broadcast ministries in the world today, reaching millions with the gospel of grace. Joseph is also the bestselling author of *The Power of Right Believing* and *Destined to Reign*, and a highly sought-after conference speaker. For more information about his other inspiring resources, visit www.JosephPrince.com.